BUILD YOUR OWN
CUSTOM CLOSET

Designing, Building & Installing Custom Closet Systems

Creative Publishing
international

CHANHASSEN, MINNESOTA
www.creativepub.com

**Creative Publishing
international**

Copyright © 2007
Creative Publishing international, Inc.
18705 Lake Drive East
Chanhassen, Minnesota 55317
1-800-328-3895
www.creativepub.com

Printed in China

10 9 8 7 6 5 4 3 2 1

Library of Congress Cataloging-in-Publication Data

Cole, Gillett,
  Build your own custom closet : designing, building & installing custom
closet systems / by Gillett Cole & Jim Myers.
    p. cm.
  Summary: "Includes detailed step-by-step instructions for 12 different
styles of closet organizers"--Provided by publisher.
  Includes index. Branded by Black & Decker.
  ISBN-13: 978-1-58923-306-5 (soft cover)
  ISBN-10: 1-58923-306-9 (soft cover)
  1. Built-in furniture. 2. Clothes closets. 3. Shelving (Furniture)
4. Storage in the home. I. Myers, Jim, II. Title.

  TT197.5.B8C585 2007
  684.1'6—dc22

2007012535

President/CEO: Ken Fund
VP for Sales & Marketing: Peter Ackroyd

Home Improvement Group

Publisher: Bryan Trandem
Managing Editor: Tracy Stanley
Senior Editor: Mark Johanson
Editor: Jennifer Gehlhar

Creative Director: Michele Lanci-Altomare
Senior Design Manager: Brad Springer
Design Managers: Jon Simpson, Mary Rohl

Director of Photography: Tim Himsel
Lead Photographer: Steve Galvin
Photo Coordinators: Julie Caruso, Joanne Wawra
Shop Manager: Bryan McLain

Production Managers: Laura Hokkanen, Linda Halls

Page Layout Artist: Kristine Mudd
Photographers: Andrea Rugg, Joel Schnell
Shop Help: Glenn Austin, John Webb

Authors: Gillett Cole, Jim Meyers
Technical Review: Michael Popowski, Philip Schmidt

BUILD YOUR OWN CUSTOM CLOSET
Created by: The Editors of Creative Publishing international, Inc., in cooperation with Black & Decker.
Black & Decker® is a trademark of The Black & Decker Corporation and is used under license.

NOTICE TO READERS

For safety, use caution, care and good judgment when following the procedures described in this book. The Publisher and Black & Decker cannot assume responsibility for any damage to property or injury to persons as a result of misuse of the information provided.

The techniques shown in this book are general techniques for various applications. In some instances, additional techniques not shown in this book may be required. Always follow manufacturers' instructions included with products, since deviating from the directions may void warranties. The projects in this book vary widely as to skill levels required: some may not be appropriate for all do-it-yourselfers, and some may require professional help.

Consult your local Building Department for information on building permits, codes and other laws as they apply to your project.

Contents

Build Your Own Custom Closet

Considering Closets

Life is ever changing. Wouldn't it be nice if your closet changed with your lifestyle? Well, wish no longer. Custom closets are modular, and with modularity comes versatility. The modular innovation phenomenon, or better known as the "custom closet phenomenon," has been around since the 1970s. In this book we'll explore both traditional and contemporary (modular) approaches to installing the perfect closet for your specific needs. The traditional building techniques incorporate standard joinery methods and well-known materials—namely wood and plywood—while the new methods use melamine and specialty modular hardware. By "modular" we mean adjustable. Adjustability is achieved with European design (most notably in hardware and fasteners).

One of the biggest drawbacks to standard rod-and-shelf closets is that they don't maximize the vertical space of your wall. In a typical closet with an 8-foot ceiling, that's a tremendous amount of wasted space. Custom closets, on the other hand, do take advantage of this precious wall space by using a practice known as "double hanging." By stacking (or double hanging) your clothes, you free up wall space for more storage. With more hanging and storage space available to you, you have the ability to have a place for everything and everything in its place.

Custom closets don't just have to be about function and utility. We spend much time and money decorating our bedrooms and living spaces. Why should our closets be any different? Consider using products that match the rest of the hardware and wood finishes in your home. If nothing else, you can take great comfort knowing a custom closet protects the sizeable investment you make in your wardrobe. When items have a designated hanging spot or are folded neatly on a shelf, they look better and last longer. While function and utility are important, appearance can be just as important with custom closets.

Inspiration

Knowing exactly what you want to store in your closet helps with the initial planning and designing stages. By using modular units and adjustable shelving, you can adjust your closest to fit your needs over time. In this section we'll share with you the closet systems, styles, and features that have made the contemporary closet the new Rolls-Royce in home design.

A creative way to maximize your closet space using both a wall-hung and floor-based system. The floor-based system expands storage from floor to ceiling, while the wall-hung section allows space below for hanging clothes and extra floor storage as needed.

Here's a nice illustration of how closet accessories are becoming more innovative as the custom closet industry matures and becomes more sophisticated.

With a contemporary feel, this floor-based closet system offers a nice balance of hanging and shelving. The mirrored effect the closet has makes for equal his and hers space, keeping sides well defined while also orderly and neat.

For those who truly want the best in function, materials, and design, this closet is loaded! With features such as designer glass, crown molding, a hidden ironing board, raised drawer fronts, and a center island, this closet feels more like a room than a closet.

This beautiful maple wall-hung closet system makes the most out of this reach-in closet. The double-hang section is smartly mounted on the return wall to make the hanging clothes more accessible.

For those with a sophisticated modern palette, this closet is for you. With its impressive blend of steel wall rails, bright orange drawers, and dark wood veneer cabinet doors—not to mention the recessed lights and matching wall paint—here's a closet that would make Frank Lloyd Wright proud.

Don't forget—or underestimate the importance of—the doors. Closet doors add design chic to any room. Here, these simple sliding doors add visual punch to an entire wall.

Sliding doors are a decorative option for smaller closet spaces as well. Translucent doors allow the light of the closet to be shared with the accompanying room without personal items being on display.

Simple bifold closet doors have the ability to make a design statement within any room. With some thought, your closet doors can reflect your personal style and add elegance to the room. Think of your door as a large piece of artwork hung on the wall.

This contemporary Euro-design closet system, with its stunning wood veneer finish and wardrobe lighting, is just the closet for finer attire that you want to protect.

Not just for clothing storage anymore, custom closets are perfect for pantries, too. This well-designed pantry makes the most of the space by offering smart storage solutions for dry goods, with roll-out chrome baskets, adjustable shelves for bottled and canned goods, vertical panels for cooking and baking ware, and lovely wine racks for your favorite merlot.

Sick of having your clothes resemble the Leaning Tower of Pisa? Here's the benefit of having adjustable shelves. These blonde melamine adjustable shelves are versatile enough to store storage boxes, hats, and purses neatly and properly.

Can you say Utopia?
This closet offers utility and elegance all in one design. There are horizontal fixed shelves running all along the bottom and top, and crown molding along the top for a built-in appeal. The natural light of the window is preserved without sacrificing the storage space below.

This home office is a fine example of how custom closets transcend wardrobe closets and become so much more. This home office design nicely incorporates the needs of the home— by offering adjustable linen shelves—with the needs of the professional working from home—by offering hanging and base cabinets and a beautiful peninsula countertop.

To maximize a typical reach-in kid's closet add triple-hang, adjustable shelves, and rollout baskets.

Part of the custom feel of closets is achieved from attention to details. Carefully choose wall colors, shelf materials, and accessories.

A mother's dream! If you want your kids to put their clothes away, you need to provide the right closet—and this nice floor-based closet system does just that. With its angled shoe shelves, drawers, and double-hang sections, your teenager will gladly hang up clothes and keep shoes in order.

This closet, with its maple laminate shelves and drawer fronts, also uses a metal track system to offer adjustability while saving on costs.

If budget is a concern, here is a creative and affordable way to offer double-hang using a metal track system, while also using a white laminate shoe cubby and drawer section.

Planning

Much is expected of contemporary closets. They need to be adjustable for our ever-changing lifestyles, but they also need to be sturdy, reliable, and affordable. To achieve all of this, there are preferred materials, hardware, and fasteners used by closet installers. Many products are available at home centers, and the specialty products are available through online or catalog resources (see Resources). These specialty products are becoming more readily available in home centers as more DIYers see the cost benefit of designing and building their own closet systems. In this section we'll discuss the basic components of closet systems and the options you have to build them.

In this section:

- Closet Overview
- Materials
- Trim & Molding
- Accessories
- Tools, Hardware & Fasteners
- Survey the Closet Space
- Identify Obstructions
- Choose a Closet System

Closet Overview

Before we get started it's important to understand just how much closet building has evolved. Traditionally, a closet system was constructed with a ¾"-thick sheet of plywood and a few feet of 1 × 3 lumber. In this system, "sections" (the space between any two verticals) must be completely constructed and then set into place—shelves are nailed in between verticals for a sturdy box, in essence, that is most stable when resting on the floor. To build around this section, top shelves or shelf cleats rest upon wall supports (called "nailers"). The top shelves are lowered on top of the nailer and nailed in place along the top of the verticals. We use this basic method as an alternative to the wall-hung project, but we update it slightly by incorporating modular hardware—which adds structural support to the entire unit, and in turn allows for some of the fixed, supportive shelves to be replaced with adjustable shelves.

The major advantage closets today have is increased adjustability. A modular closet system consists of verticals and shelves just as its predecessor. The verticals either stand on the floor (a "floor-based" system) or hang on a wall rail (a "wall-hung" system). Wall-hung systems have evolved greatly thanks to modular hanging rail systems. Traditionally, each section had to be assembled and then lifted into place.

While holding the section in place, each shelf cleat had to be fastened to the wall. With modular innovations, the weight burden of the unit is distributed more to the verticals (not just the shelf cleats). The verticals have brackets fastened to them that allow you to hang all of the verticals on the wall, and then you continue to fill in the sections; you have the ability to adjust verticals to plumb at any time. This has transformed closet installation into a single-person job.

Modular closets have shelving that is fixed and adjustable. Fixed shelves are fastened to the wall with cleats or steel L-brackets, and they are often fastened to other shelves through the verticals with modular hardware (see page 22), thus providing structural reinforcement to the entire unit by distributing weight loads from section to section.

In any closet system a single wall is called a "unit," and each unit consists of sections. The units in a walk-in closet are joined in the corners (see Installing Corner Units starting on page 50). Custom cabinetry experience comes in handy at this stage. Finally, in each section accessories are added based on your personal storage needs—such as baskets, drawers, rods, shoe cubbies, and vertical spacers.

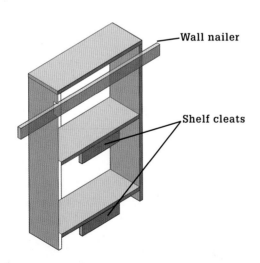

With a traditional closet system each section is constructed and then lifted into place on the wall. The verticals are notched to rest on a nailer, helping you hold the section in place as shelf cleats are screwed to the wall. This process requires two installers.

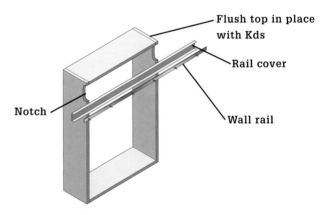

Modular closets offer a much more efficient installation process. Adjustable brackets are fastened to verticals, and then verticals are hung on rails along the wall. As verticals are supported by the rail, the installer has free hands to build out each section, adjusting to plumb and level throughout the installation process. L-brackets are then fastened to fixed shelves, and occasionally under verticals. This process is practical for a single installer.

Materials

Today melamine shelving stock is the preferred material for verticals and shelves. It is widely available, inexpensive, and comes in a host of colors and faux wood finishes. Cost is the major factor that has led closet installers to use melamine: this inexpensive yet durable material allows for other custom features to be added to the closet unit while still staying on budget.

Most home centers carry melamine shelving stock or MDF board suitable for the projects in this book; however, custom closet companies will often purchase industrial strength, high-density melamine (for a slightly higher cost) to ensure the greatest durability. These dense versions can often be special ordered from home centers or lumberyards (density is often specified in board manufacturers' data sheets).

Precut stock is available at most home centers in ¾" thicknesses and in standard depths of 12", 14", 16", and 18" (larger depths are often available should you happen to have a large return wall and desire deep shelving). The stock is also available with predrilled shelf-pin holes. MDF board and melamine sheets allow you to cut verticals and shelves to custom sizes. They are often sold as ¾"-thick, 4 × 8' sheets.

Plywood is another option for closets verticals and shelves, but it is typically more expensive and does not offer the host of finishes available in melamine.

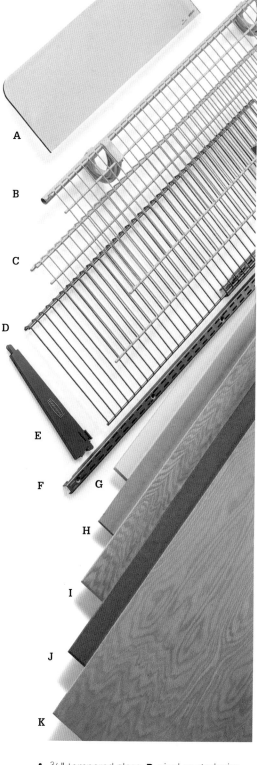

A. ¾" × 12 × 8' melamine shelf stock with predrilled holes,
B. ¾" × 16 × 8' melamine shelf stock with predrilled holes,
C. ¾" melamine shelf stock without predrilled holes,
D. ¾" finish-grade oak shelving, **E.** ¾" melamine shelving with faux wood finish.

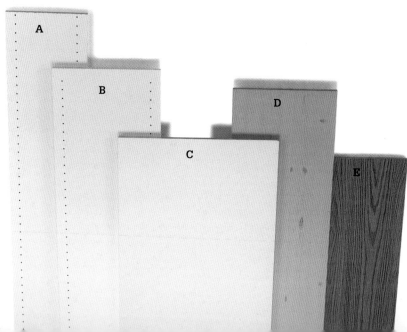

A. ⅜" tempered glass, **B.** vinyl-coated wire shelving with hanger space, **C.** standard vinyl-coated wire shelving, **D.** metal wire shelving, **E.** brackets, **F.** metal wall standards, **G.** ¾" × 4 × 8' melamine sheet, **H.** ½" oak plywood, **I.** ¾" finish-grade oak plywood, **J.** ¾" × 4 × 8' MDF board sheet, **K.** ½" × 4 × 8' MDF board sheet.

For a more finished look, you have the option to paint or finish plywood with tinted oils or stains. For built-ins, finish-grade plywood is often used for exposed areas, and it is usually edged with hardwood strips or moldings. Finish-grade plywood (oak or birch) is often used for interiors of built-ins; it is made from several layers of softwood veneer sandwiched between hardwood surface veneers.

For shelving that requires little weight and has a short span (such as shoe cubby inserts), ½"-thick MDF sheets are available. For adjustable shelving consider tempered glass, which is great for decorative shelving that is not intended to hold much weight. Standard glass shelving (12 × 12) rests on adjustable pins. The span should be 24" or less. Glass shelving is sold at most home centers.

Wire shelving is yet another material used for closet organization, and it is widely available. There are two basic types available: vinyl-coated and metal—the metal typically being the more industrial of the two and therefore predominantly used in sheds, basements, and garages. Wire shelving is also available with a space for hangers.

Finally, systems that use metal standards are widely available and inexpensive shelving options. They are easy to install, and their simple, industrial style has made them the preferred choice for garage organization.

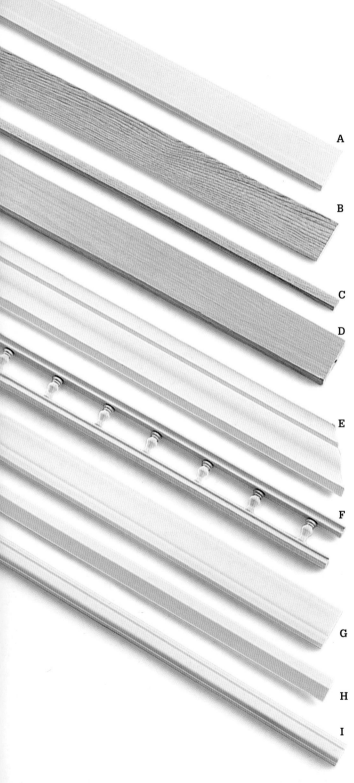

Trim & Molding

Trim moldings are both decorative and functional. They can be used to cover gaps around the base and sides of floor-based and built-in closets, to hide the edges of plywood and melamine surfaces, or simply to add visual interest to a project. Moldings are available in dozens of styles. Synthetic trim moldings, made of wood composites or rigid foam covered with a layer of melamine, are less expensive than hardwood moldings. For face frames, hardwood strips are used (available in 1 × 2, 1 × 3, or 1 × 4 sizes).

Baseboard molding and base shoe molding is used to trim the bottom edge (along the floor line) of a floor-based or built-in closet, while crown and cove moldings cover gaps between the top of a closet and the ceiling.

Other molding you may use is door-edge ("cap" molding to create panel-style doors and drawer faces), shelf-edge ("base cap" molding to give a decorative edge to shelves), and ornamental (used as a decorative accent, especially on slanted shoe shelves).

A. melamine face frame, **B.** solid oak face frame (1 × 3), **C.** base shoe molding, **D.** crown molding, **E.** baseboard molding, **F.** decorative molding, **G.** synthetic trim molding, **H.** shelf-edge molding, **I.** synthetic trim molding.

Accessories

When it comes to accessories, what's available at your local home center greatly influences your overall design. For example, preassembled drawers, baskets, and shelving stock all come in standard sizes. To make your closet designs coincide with the accessory sizes most available in your area, make a quick trip to the storage supplies section of your local home center. Of course, you can build your own custom accessories (for drawers and shelves, especially). Be sure to measure any accessory you plan to buy—prepackaged items often have nominal measurements on the packaging. For example, baskets are often sized nominally and therefore do not need clearance added to the space required for them in your design, while drawers usually require a 1" clearance in your design. If ordering accessories online ask a representative for the actual and nominal measurements, so you can accurately design your closet. Standard drawer sizes include 16 × 10", 25 × 5", and 25 × 10". Standard basket widths are 16 and 24", standard depths are 12 and 14", and standard heights are 5 and 10".

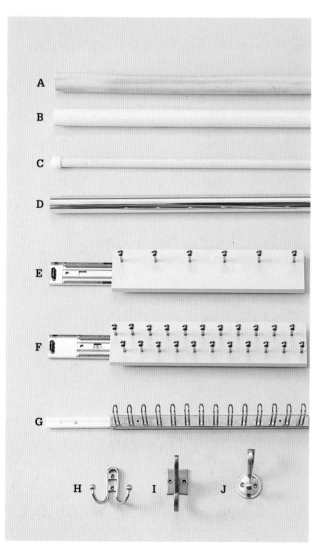

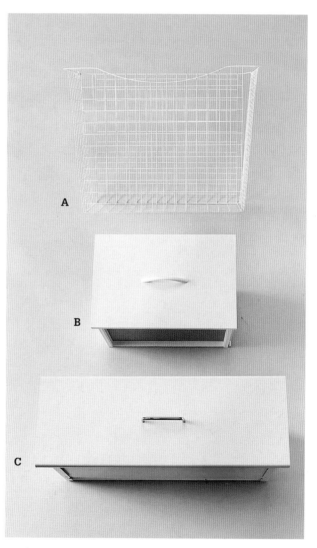

A. wood dowel/closet rod, **B.** plastic closet rod, **C.** small, plastic closet rod, **D.** steel closet rod, **E.** glide-out belt rack, **F.** glide-out tie rack, **G.** tie/belt rack, **H.** double wall hook, **I.** and **J.** single wall hooks.

A. wire basket, **B.** and **C.** preassembled melamine drawers.

Tools, Hardware & Fasteners

Regardless of the type of closet system you install, there are common hardware, fasteners, and tools you'll use when building your custom closet. Your blade types for saws should be appropriate for the type of material you're using. An alternate-tooth blade configuration and high grind angle make for clean cuts on MDF and melamine.

A. circular saw (with melamine blade for melamine applications), **B.** brad nailer/stapler, **C.** cordless nailer, **D.** drill press, **E.** finish nailer, **F.** table saw, **G.** stud finder/laser level, **H.** household iron, **I.** plumb bob, **J.** angle finder, **K.** framing square, **L.** hacksaw, **M.** flashlight, **N.** Torpedo level, **O.** hammer, **P.** rubber mallet, **Q.** prybar, **R.** level, **S.** nail puller, **T.** paint scraper, **U.** putty knife, **V.** pliers, **W.** needlenose pliers, **X.** painter's tape, **Y.** masking tape, **Z.** tape measure, **AA.** drill bits, **BB.** 20 mm and ¾" drill bits, **CC.** 5 mm drill bits, **DD.** flush-cutting bit, **EE.** router bit, **FF.** reverse-thread screw extractor bit, **GG.** utility knife, **HH.** spade bit, **II.** nailset, **JJ.** Phillips screwdriver, **KK.** flathead screwdriver, **LL.** ½" wood chisel, **MM.** ¾" wood chisel, **NN.** 1" wood chisel, **OO.** cordless drill/driver, **PP.** router, **QQ.** drill, **RR.** jigsaw (with melamine blade for melamine applications).

Standard Hardware & Fasteners

Standard hardware and fasteners are often used in conjunction with the specialty hardware (on page 22). For traditional closet systems (namely built-ins), everything you need is here.

Typical closet installation requires wood screws for studs, drywall screws for drywall, and Euro or barrel screws and knock-down (KD) screws/dowels for use within the shelving material. When choosing screws for anchors, match the screw thread to that of the anchor. Also check the maximum fixture thickness to ensure the screw is long enough to go through your material and fasten into the anchor.

*not actual size

A. 10d finish nail, B. 8d finish nail, C. 6d finish nail, D. 4d finish nail, E. 1¼" drywall screw, F. ¾" drywall screw, G. 1⅝" drywall screw, H. 2½" drywall screw, I. and J. toggle bolts, K. ¾" panhead screw, L. and M. wood screws, N. 1¼" panhead screw, O. steel L-brackets ("corner" brackets), P. wood glue, Q. melamine glue, R. door hinges for cabinets, S. shims, T. metal shelf standards, U. mending plate, V. biscuits, W. door knobs, X. edgebanding tape, Y. drawer pulls, Z. metal shelf brackets, AA. shelf pegs and pins, BB. wood dowels.

Specialty Hardware & Fasteners

Contemporary modular units now use locking-cam hardware. Hardware manufacturers often call these parts "KDs" (knock-down fittings), while closet companies and prepackaged closet manufacturers call them "cams" or "locking cams." When making your own custom closet, search hardware manufacturers for KDs, KD screws, and KD screw and dowels (see Resources).

The KD screw and dowels allow you to fasten two modular shelves together through an adjoining vertical panel, adding strength to each section and the overall unit. Using this modular hardware allows you to also have adjustable shelves set on pins, and it allows you to move or add fixed shelves (the KDs simply "unlock" with a screwdriver, allowing you to lift off the shelf).

Yet another reason modular closets are more adjustable is because adjustable hanging brackets are fastened to verticals, which are then hung on hanging rails on the wall. These brackets allow you to adjust the verticals plumb. You also can readjust the verticals as you're installing the closet system. If you have to mount shelves or a mounting rail on drywall, use anchors. For heavy loads, the anchor of choice is a Toggler bolt; for medium loads metal toggle bolts are used; for lighter loads self-drilling metal anchors or plastic anchors are used (see Resources). Shelving and most accessories are fastened to verticals with Euro or barrel screws that fit right into the predrilled shelf-pin holes of shelving stock available at home centers.

Wire Shelving Hardware & Fasteners

The hardware and fasteners for wire shelving is unique unto itself. They oftentimes are provided with wire shelving packages. However, if you purchase bulk wire shelving with the intent to cut to size according to a custom design, most home centers now carry the hardware and fasteners separately to get the job done.

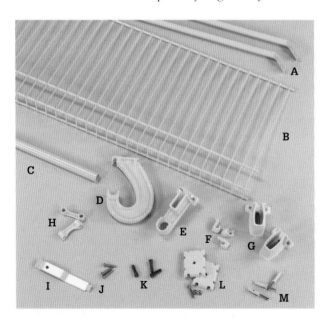

A. support brackets, **B.** vinyl-coated wire shelving, **C.** clothing rod, **D.** clothing rod hanger, **E.** side-wall support for rod, **F.** wall clips, **G.** side-wall support brackets, **H.** wire endcaps, **I.** connector bracket, **J.** manufacturer screws, **K.** wall anchors, **L.** connectors, **M.** bracket anchors.

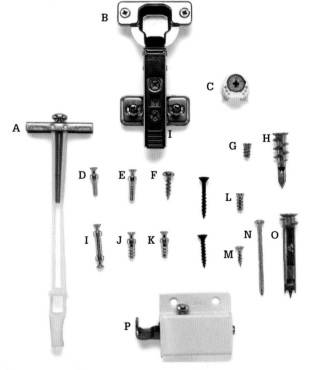

A. Toggler SnapToggle ¼-20, **B.** Euro cabinet door hinge, **C.** knock-down fitting (KD), **D.** connecting bolts (KD dowel), **E.** a single connector bolt, **F.** panhead screws, **G.** Euro screw, **H.** self-drilling anchor, **I.** double-ended bolt (KD screw/dowel connector), **J.** connecting bolt (KD screw), **K.** connecting bolt (KD screw), **L.** Euro or "barrel" screw, **M.** flathead screw, **N.** machine screw, **O.** self-drilling toggle, **P.** hanging bracket (fastened to verticals).

How to Use Toggler Bolts

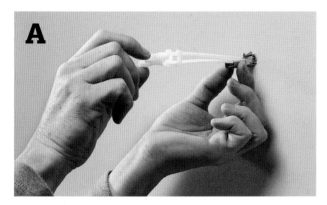

Drill a hole in the wall according to manufacturer instructions, and then insert the metal flange into it.

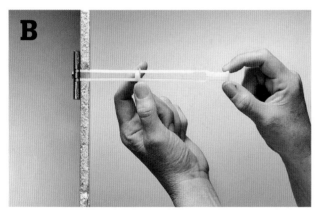

Pull the flange tight against the inside of the wall and slide the plastic ring against the front of the wall.

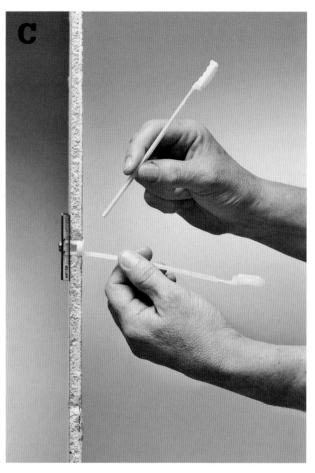

Snap off the plastic ends so the remaining anchor is flush to the wall. Drive machine screws through shelf or rail into anchor using Phillips screwdriver.

How to Use Self-drilling Metal Anchors

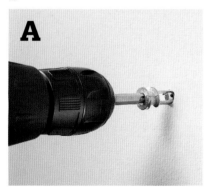

Drive the anchor into wall in between studs. As the threads touch drywall, slowly tighten the toggle until it's nearly flush to wall.

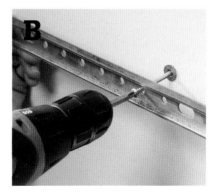

Insert a screw through rail and into anchor.

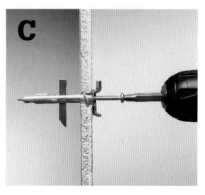

As you drive the screw into the anchor, the metal flange pulls tight against the inside of the wall.

Survey the Closet Space

The first step in building a custom closet is to come up with a design based on the planned space. The design phase is extremely important and must be accurate and thorough if you are to achieve your desired results and have a smooth installation. Here is a list of materials you will need to design your closet system:

1. Measuring tape
2. Pencil
3. Ruler or straightedge
4. Notepad
5. Graph paper with a scale

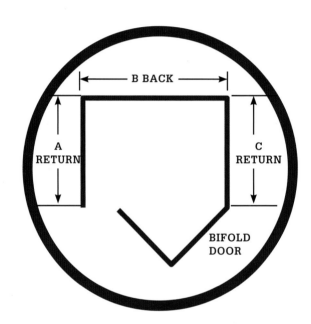

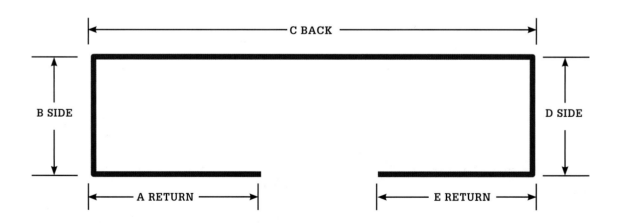

Sections are often labeled alphabetically—this helps to keep measurements organized during the design stage. Most reach-in and walk-in closets consist of return, side, and back walls. Occasionally, small reach-in closets (often placed in the home for pantry or linen needs) lack official return walls.

Measure the width and height of the door opening(s).

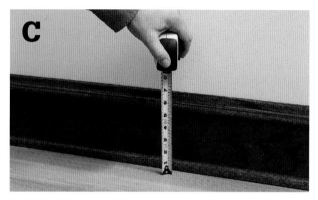

Hang a plumb bob from the ceiling and measure between the string and the wall at several locations to check for bowed or irregular walls. Measure the return walls, side walls, and back wall, using a measuring tape.

Measure large and ornate molding that you intend to leave in place and work around.

How to Survey a Closet

A. MEASURING THE CLOSET SPACE

1. Using your measuring tape, measure your ceiling height. Write down all of your measurements on a notepad. If you have vaulted ceilings, make sure you measure both the lowest and highest points of the ceiling. Also, use an angle finder to determine the slope in between those two points.

2. Identify bowed or irregular walls by hanging a plumb bob from the ceiling near the work area and measuring between the string and the wall at several points. Mark the wall at the shortest distance: built-in units should be constructed so the back is plumb and flush at this point.

3. Next, measure the length of all walls, including return walls. *Note: The return wall measurement gives you the maximum depth the verticals can be. Standard shelf depths are 12", 14", 16", and 18".*

B. MEASURING FOR DOORS

1. Measure your door width and height.

2. Note the door type. It can make a difference in your design layout if you have bifold, swing, sliding, or pocket doors. *Note: Walls that contain pocket doors must be marked for the depth in which the pocket door slides into the wall (that is, any portion of the wall that includes the door cavity). This wall space cannot support wall-hung systems.*

C. MEASURING BASE MOLDING

Finally, measure the height and depth of your base molding. This is necessary if you plan to notch around the molding or keep a wall-hung unit above the molding. *Note: If base molding does not need to remain in place and is an obstacle for a floor-based system or built-in (see page 16), remove it.*

Identify Obstructions

Identifying obstructions in your design can make the difference between a weekend installation and a week-long installation. Some typical obstructions you will find in a closet are: light switches, outlets, ventilation ducts, pipes, electrical panels, overhead lights, and sprinkler systems. It's important to measure these obstructions, allow for space according to local codes, and incorporate this information into your overall design. You don't want to find out during installation that a vertical panel is going to hit an outlet or cover a heating vent, for example.

Also check for pipes, ducts, wood blocking, or other obstructions inside your walls. A quality stud finder will help with this. Studs are often placed 16" apart, so if your stud finder picks up on something in between that, avoid drilling holes in that area. Plumbing is usually routed along walls with toilets or sinks, so take extra precaution if you're working in a closet that shares a wall with these items on the other side.

Remove baseboards and other moldings to make room for a built-in or floor-based system that will fit flush against the wall. Use a flat pry bar with a wood block to prevent damage to the wall, and pry carefully to avoid splintering the molding. (Inset) Move electrical receptacles and other fixtures, if they are in the way of your planned design. You also may need to add receptacles. *Note: If you are not experienced at working with wiring, hire an electrician to do this work.*

Pipes or sprinklers may be harder to re-route than work around. Be sure to check with local building codes to determine the required space to leave open around sprinklers, pipes, and outlets. Measure and mark lines around these obstacles.

Measure the distance wall lights are hung from the corner. If your planned vertical depth is greater than this space, your unit cannot hang verticals flush into the corner.

Choose a Closet System

Now that you have measured your space and identified possible obstructions, you'll want to determine which system is right for your space—built-in, floor-based, or wall-hung systems are the three most common choices when it comes to custom designs. Usually in new homes, any system will work. It's more a matter of personal taste. However, in an older home, wall-hung systems are preferable because you don't have to worry if the floors and walls are uneven. Wall-hung systems hang on a wall track, using brackets that can be adjusted for a plumb installation despite an imperfect wall.

Wall-hung units hang on a track, so perfectly level floors are not required. However, if the tracks do not offer adjustability, irregular walls must be accurately measured and all verticals and cleats must be adjusted to these measurements for a plumb installation.

Wall Hung: Pros	Wall Hung: Cons
• Easy to install	• Weight limitations
• Easy to make level, even if floors and walls are not square	• Depth limitations
• No notching around baseboards	• Doesn't have built-in look
• Nice clean, contemporary look with everything off the floor	
• Allows removal or cleaning of closet flooring	

A floor-based unit adds extra storage, but is more difficult to level on uneven floors. For slight inconsistencies, wood shims can be used under the units. Notch around large baseboards.

Floor Based: Pros	Floor Based: Cons
• Minimal weight limitations	• More difficult installation
• Allows for deeper shelving	• Harder to level if floors and walls are not square
• Has built-in look and feel	• Need to remove or notch around baseboards
	• More difficult to replace and clean closet flooring
	• Mildly difficult to tear out

Built-ins are permanently joined to the structure of the house. They add a custom look to your home and allow you to use awkward or wasted spaces.

Built-in: Pros	Built-in: Cons
• Sturdy and permanent appearance	• Difficult installation
• Minimal weight limitation	• Typically constructed with more expensive wood materials
• Allows for deeper shelving	• Cannot replace or clean flooring unless unit is torn out
	• Very difficult to tear out

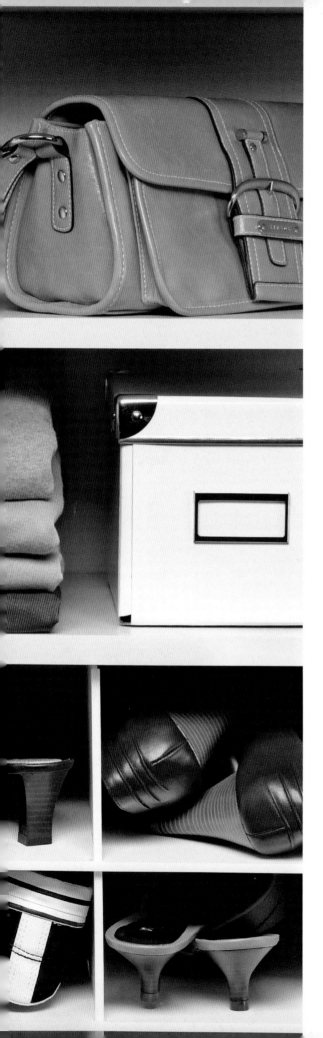

Design

For many people the design stage is the most enjoyable. It is the time when you start to look at materials and custom options. It is a time to truly inspect your items and the space you have to store those items. The more time spent up front inspecting and designing, the smoother the installation will be later.

In this section:

- Take Inventory
- Graph Your Custom Design
- Determine Materials Needed & Cut Lists
- Sample Designs

Take Inventory

After you survey your closet space and determine which system is right for your space, it's time to determine what you want to accomplish with the closet. Ninety percent of closets are used for wardrobe storage, so we will explain the design steps for that usage now. The same basic methods can be applied to other types of closets. First make a list of all the items you plan on putting back into your closet. Here is a quick reference guide to help you make an inventory list:

1. How much short-hang do you need?
2. How much long-hang do you need?
3. How much medium-hang (or pants by the cuff) do you need?
4. How much shelf storage do you need?
5. How much drawer space do you need?

Long-, medium-, and short-hang classification is determined by the sizes of your clothing and how you like to store that clothing. Separate clothing and items into categories by likeness. For example, hang all of the long-hanging items together on a rod (followed by medium hang and short hang). Then fold and stack all of the sweaters you intend to store on shelves, all of your shoes, and all of your hobby supplies (items not part of your wardrobe that you'd like to fit into your closet). See the chart on this page for guidelines on how clothing is typically categorized.

To ensure your folded items remain neat on shelves, plan on stacking bulky sweaters in groups of three or four and T-shirts or thinner clothing in stacks of five or six.

Checklist ▶

Here is a checklist to help you walk through the inventory survey process. Be sure to take note of frequently used items and reserve easy-access locations for them.

Item	(W × D × H)	Quantity	Space Needed
Shelves			
Shoes			
Sweaters and bulky shirts			
Folded items			
Seasonal clothing (top shelf or drawers)			
T-shirts (or drawers)			
Hats			
Purses			
Large objects (luggage, for example)			
Long-hang			
Dress pants (by the cuff)			
Long skirts			
Long dresses			
Medium-hang			
Dress shirts			
Pants (folded)			
Short-hang			
Shorts (folded, or fold and store in drawers)			
Short skirts			
Short dresses			
Drawers or Baskets			

How to Take Inventory

A. DETERMINE HANGING SPACE

1. Measure the linear feet of your hanging clothes. This gives you the minimum amount of space needed.
2. Decipher how much short hang is needed and how much long hang is needed. If you hang your pants by the cuff, then you need to design a medium-hang section. If you fold them over hangers, then you can design a double-hang section.

B. DETERMINE SHELVING SPACE

1. Determine how many linear or cubic feet of shelving is needed for sweaters and folded clothes.
2. Count the shoes and purses. Be sure to separate out any irregular items, like tall boots, and count them separately.
3. Determine the maximum height needed for each category of shelving items. For example, 24 shoes @ 6", 6 boots @ 12". Standard shelves are 12" to 13" in height. As a general rule of thumb, add 3" to the height of your object for actual shelving height. The extra space allows for easy access to the items.

C. REVIEW & DETERMINE ACCESSORY SPACE

1. Lastly, do you want to incorporate drawers and baskets into the closet? Consider adding some kind of laundry solution, like a hamper, and drawers, especially for socks and undergarments. You also may like to add a jewelry insert into one of the drawers (typically the top drawer and a slightly smaller version than other drawers). Estimate the needed space for these items. Often you can determine if your sock pile is big enough to fill a 30 × 12 × 12" drawer or if you need something deeper. Or if you prefer to add sock inserts, you'll have to spread your socks out more, requiring less depth but perhaps more drawers.
2. Now it's time for the design review. This is when you revisit which closet system is best not only for your space (which sometimes limits which system you use), but also which system is best for your items. A floor-based system, for example, instantly gives you more storage space because shelving and drawers extend to the floor. Now is also the time to finalize your materials and finishes. Do you want maple, cherry, or white shelving? Do you want to add crown molding or have toe-kicks?

Measure the total (minimum) linear feet of hanging space you'll need based on the existing hanging items in your closet.

Measure the total (minimum) linear feet of shelving you'll need to accommodate the items you plan to store in the closet.

Take inventory of other items you'll want to store in the closet. Determine what types (and approximate sizes) of accessories you'll need.

Graph Your Custom Design

Now that you have surveyed your closet space and your clothing inventory, it's time to design your closets. Use graph paper with a scale of your choosing (e.g., one box on the graph will represent 2") to create two plans for each closet. The first is a floor plan. The floor plan is a bird's-eye view of the closet. It lays out the overall dimensions of the space and exhibits the depths of the closet components.

The second is an elevation plan. This is the place to add custom features to the design. For example, wall A may consist of single and double hanging, while wall B may include drawers, shoe shelves, and a space for long hanging. In the elevation plan, the detail of each wall is laid out. In each elevation plan, identify wall heights and widths as well as detail all the closet components and accessories—including the height and width of the entire closet system.

Be sure to include the thickness of all vertical panels in your overall dimensions. A typical vertical panel is ¾" thick. This amount must be accounted for when determining the lengths of the shelves. If you are using four vertical panels in your design, make sure to account for those 3" in your overall scheme.

FLOOR PLAN

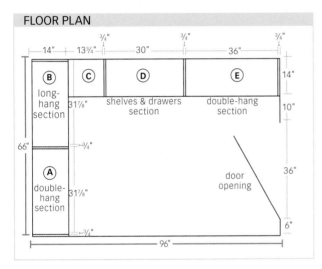

Use scaled graph paper to create a basic floor plan. Be sure to leave space for obstacles, according to local codes.

Measuring Tip ▸

These tips will help you design a closet in a way that makes the most of your space.

- Divide hanging spaces into two sections to maximize hanging space and free up wall space for drawers and shelves.
- In reach-in closets, it's best to place drawers or baskets in the middle of the closet, so return walls won't prevent drawers from opening.
- In narrow walk-in closets, it's best to have shelving sections on the left and right walls placed near the door opening and your hanging sections closer to the back wall. Hangers usually stick out 22" from the wall, so having shelving (instead of hangers) near the door opening will prevent you from bumping into the hangers as you enter your closet.

ELEVATION PLAN

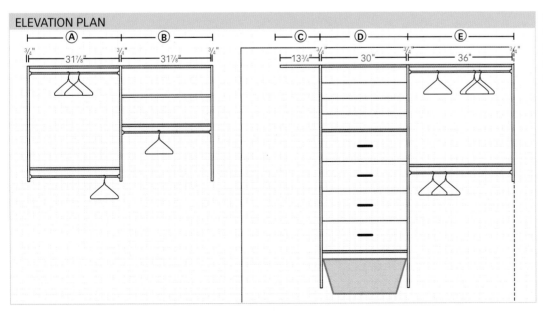

Using the same type of graph paper, add the custom features in an elevation plan.

Determine Materials Needed and Cut Lists

Now that you have your floor plans and elevation plans drawn, it's time to figure out exactly what you need and how much of it you need. Refer to the list on page 30. Here is a sample materials list based on the elevation plan on page 32.

The cut list consists of the actual dimensions for all of your finished, cut pieces. Your plans show the total height of the closet. The height of the unit is drawn to scale. For systems that use a nailer or hanging rail there is also a "mounting height," which is typically not shown on plans. This is the height at which the bottom of the rail should be aligned. Installing the rail at that point allows the top of the finished system to rest 84" high. A lower mounting height may be needed if a different end height is desired. Follow rail and bracket manufacturer instructions. Determine the mounting height by subtracting the width of the nailer or rail (and shelf cleats, if you're using them along the underside of top shelves) from the desired closet height. Here is an example cut list based on the elevation plan on page 32.

EXAMPLE: Tools, Materials & Cutting List ▶

(7) Verticals: Melamine shelf stock
$\frac{3}{4}$" × 8' × 14"
(6) Shelves: Melamine shelf stock
$\frac{3}{4}$" × 8' × 14"
Alternative to 8' stock shelves is to buy melamine sheets, cut to size, and drill all shelf-pin holes along verticals
(3) Closet rods with cups 31⅞"
(2) Closet rods with cups 36"
(4) Pre-built drawers
30" × 12" × 10", nominal
(1) Basket on track system
30" × 14" × 10", nominal

Key	Part	Dimension	Pcs. Material
A	Mounting height	81" (Actual height of system is 84")	
B	Verticals	40"	4
C	Verticals	31 ⁹⁄₁₆"	3
D	Shelves	31⅞"	5
E	Shelves	14"	1
F	Shelves	13¾"	1
G	Shelves	30"	5
H	Shelves	36"	2
I	Closet rods (with cups)	76"	2
J	Closet rods (with cups)	35 ¹¹⁄₁₆"	2
K	Drawers	28 × 14 × 10", actual	
L	Basket	28 × 14 × 1", actual	

Tip: How to Determine Actual Measured Height ▶

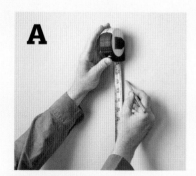

Measure up to 81" and mark a level line on the wall.

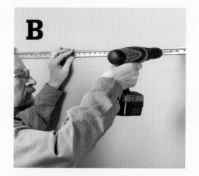

Align the bottom of the wall rail with the level line on wall, and fasten to wall with a few screws.

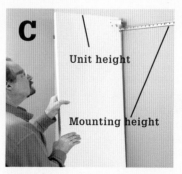

Set vertical in place with bracket over rail.

Sample Designs

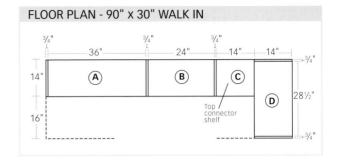

FLOOR PLAN - 90" x 30" WALK IN

With a small walk-in closet it is often best to have the connector shelf on the longest wall. In this example, the back wall has the connector shelf to maximize the storage potential on the 30"-long side wall. This takes advantage of the extra 8" of wall space on the side wall (the back wall space available is 28" long). In small closets, every inch counts!

SECTIONS:
A - Double-hang Section
B - Shelves, Drawers, and Basket
C - Corner Connection with Long-hang (D)
D - Shelves and Long-hang Section

SPECIFICATIONS:
Short-hang = 36"
Medium-hang = 36"
Long-hang = 30"
Shelves = 156"
Basket = 1 @ 24"
Drawers = 4 @ 24" ea.

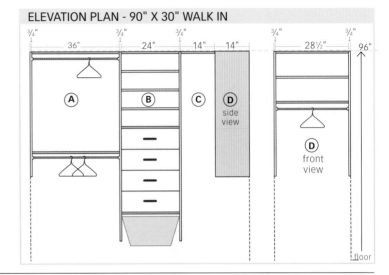

ELEVATION PLAN - 90" X 30" WALK IN

Keep sections with baskets or premade drawers the same size in each section to make product shopping (or construction) easier. Stop by your local store before designing to see what sizes and styles are available. If your closet has double bifold doors, there is a section in the middle of your closet that is going to be hard to reach. Measure this space and incorporate it into your design. It is best used as hanging space, so you can slide items hid behind the doors into easier access. Other storage options—such as shelving—will be more cumbersome when it comes to retrieving items from this space.

SECTIONS:
A - Double-hang Section
B - Shelves, Drawers, and Basket
C - Shelves and Long-hang Section
D - Shelves, Drawers, and Basket
E - Double-hang Section

SPECIFICATIONS:
Short-hang = 30"
Medium-hang = 102"
Long-hang = 31½"
Shelves = 260"
Basket = 2 @ 24"
Drawers = 6 @ 24" ea.

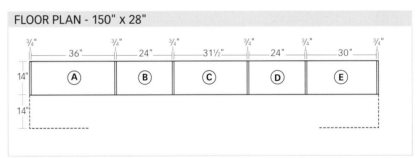

FLOOR PLAN - 150" x 28"

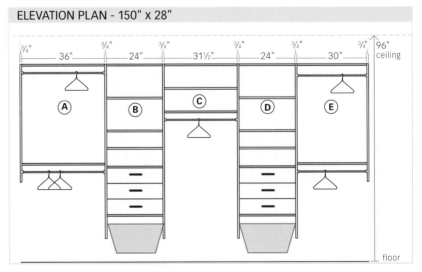

ELEVATION PLAN - 150" x 28"

FLOOR PLAN - 140" x 60" TUNNEL CLOSET

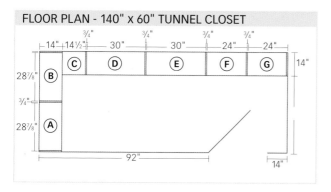

Every so often a designer has to contend with a difficult layout. One of the most common non-typical closets is a "tunnel closet." This closet has a longer wall section along one side of the door opening. A closet can be considered a tunnel closet if the longer return wall is twice as long as the other door-side wall (or at least 10" longer from the end wall to the door molding). One potential solution for a tunnel closet is to position the hanging sections along the side walls of the closet. This configuration will maximize your hanging and will also give you better access to your clothing.

ELEVATION PLAN - 140" x 60" TUNNEL CLOSET

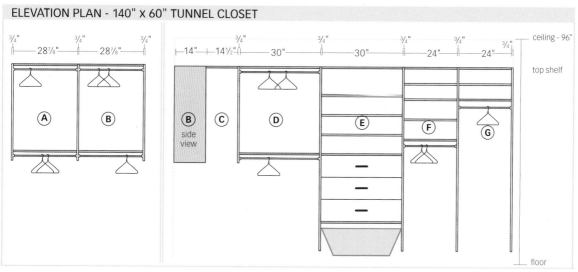

SECTIONS:
A - Double-hang Section
B - Double-hang Section
C - Corner Connection with Long-hang (B)
D - Double-hang Section
E - Shelves, Drawers, and Basket
F - Shelves and Medium-hang
G - Sheves and Long-hang

SPECIFICATIONS:
Short-hang = 87½"
Medium-hang = 111½"
Long-hang = 24"
Shelves = 264"
Basket = 1 @ 30"
Drawers = 3 @ 30" ea.

ELEVATION PLAN - 48" x 28" ENTRYWAY CLOSET

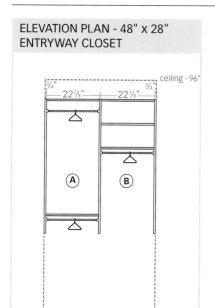

FLOOR PLAN - 48" x 28" ENTRYWAY CLOSET

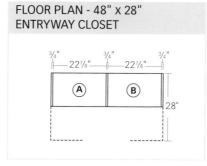

The most underutilized space is often found in entryway closets. By taking full advantage of such spaces you'll find that even the smallest closets can offer a place for your coats and your guests' coats—and maybe even some of your bulky winter clothing or seasonal rain gear! Start with this small and often ignored space, and you'll recognize the full effects of a well-organized closet.

SECTIONS:
A - Double-hang
B - Shelves and Medium-hang

SPECIFICATIONS:
Short-hang = 22⅞"
Medium-hang = 22⅞"
Long-hang = 22⅞"
Shelves = 68⅝"

Basics

This section includes detailed descriptions for all of the basic techniques that are used during a custom closet installation. It is a great starting point, and a section that you will refer to again and again.

In this section:

- Tearing Out Old Closet Material
- Adding Shelves
- Installing Corner Units
- Installing Wire Shelving
- Installing a Basic Closet Organizer
- Installing a Basic Shelving Organizer

Tearing Out Old Closet Material

To prepare the area, you must first tear out existing material. Wire shelving is the most common to remove because it is the standard shelving added to closets for new construction and for resale homes. Other systems that you may want to remove are wall-hung or floor-based units. There are a variety of reasons for why you would remove an existing unit and start over from scratch, namely for a customized closet specific to your needs. All of the removals follow the same basic procedures and require standard tools. There are instructions in the floor-based system removal that are relevant to removing a built-in, too.

Tip ▶

Lay down a moving blanket just outside of the closet. This will prevent your floors from getting dirty from the removed closet materials. Set a bucket on the blanket for collecting removed hardware and fasteners.

Tools & Materials ▶

Phillips screwdriver
Slotted screwdriver
Drill
Prybar
Utility knife
Hammer
Putty (or wallboard) knife
Fast-drying spackle
150-grit sandpaper (for sanding spackle smooth)
Pliers
Vacuum
Wood strip or block nail set

Sponge
PVA primer
Paintbrush
Paint
Framing square
Wallboard saw or jigsaw
1¼" wallboard screws
½" wallboard (or metal thickness of existing wallboard)
Self-adhesive wallboard tape
Wood putty

How to Remove Wire Shelving

A. REMOVE SUPPORT BRACKETS & SHELF CLIPS

1. Completely remove support brackets along back wall by first removing the screws holding them in place.
2. Pull the brackets out from under the wire shelving, tilting them back toward the wall if needed.
3. Remove the shelf clips. Pull them out of the wall or pry them out with a slotted screwdriver until you can pull them out. For clips that are screwed to the wall, unscrew them with a cordless screwdriver.

B. REMOVE SHELVING

1. Flip up release clips, if they are present.
2. Unclip the wire shelves from the sidewall supports. In most cases, to do this you simply lift up on the shelves to pull them out of the supports. Follow manufacturer instructions if they are available.

C. REMOVE SIDE-WALL SUPPORTS

Use a drill or screwdriver to remove the supports fastened to side walls. For brackets that have been nailed to the wall, use a prybar to pull out the nails.

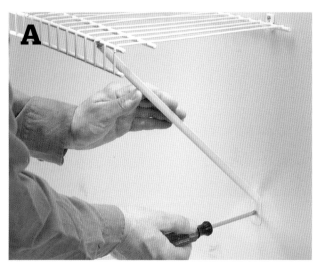

Remove the shelf clips and support brackets along the back wall using a screwdriver.

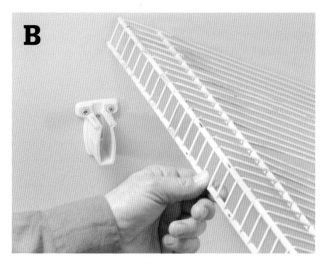

Lift up on shelving to unclip wire shelving from return wall supports. Remove all shelves.

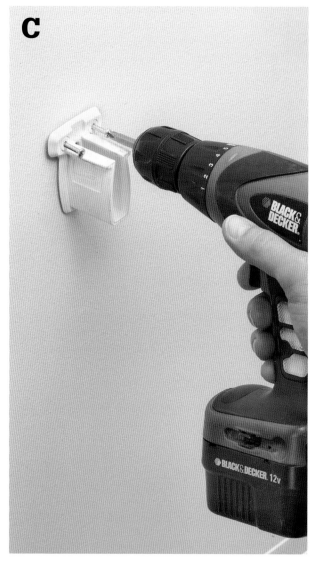

Unscrew the return wall brackets on the walls.

How to Remove a Wall-hung Unit

A. DISASSEMBLE THE UNIT

1. Remove all of the adjustable shelves by simply lifting them off the pins and pulling them out. Pull out all of the shelf pins. Set everything outside of the closet. Stacking items neatly now will make for easy re-installation or removal to the trash.
2. Starting at the top and at one end of the closet, remove L-brackets from fixed shelves (or unfasten cleats from the wall) using a drill.
3. Unlock the KDs in that same section with a screwdriver, and remove the shelf. Then remove the KD screws from the verticals. Pry out the KDs from the shelves, using a screwdriver if necessary. Repeat for each fixed shelf in that section.
4. Finally, remove the far left vertical by simply lifting it off the rail. Unscrew the rail bracket to remove it from the vertical.
5. Repeat step 3 through step 5 for the next section.
6. Repeat for each section as you move along the wall until the entire unit is disassembled.

B. REMOVE THE WALL-MOUNTING RAIL

1. Slide the fabric cover off the rail.
2. Unscrew the rail from the wall.
3. Vacuum or sweep the closet floor.

C. ALTERNATIVE: REMOVE A WALL CLEAT

1. Cut along the perimeter of the wall-mounting cleat(s) using a utility knife. This helps prevent old caulk or paint from peeling the paint or tearing the drywall paper.
2. If the cleats are fastened with screws, remove the screws. If cleats are nailed to the wall, use a pry bar to pry the cleat away from the wall.
3. Unlock KDs and lift shelf and cleat away from unit. Pry a little bit along the entire wall and repeat until the cleat is loosened.
4. Vacuum or sweep the closet floor.

Disassemble the entire unit, starting with removal of adjustable shelves, then fixed shelves and accessories, and finally verticals.

Remove the screws in the wall rail; then remove toggles. Work from the outside toward the center so you end up in the middle, where it is easiest to balance the rail and lower it from the wall.

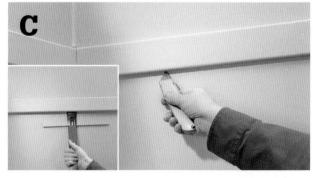

Alternative: To remove a wall cleat, first score along the edges with a utility knife, and then pry it away from the wall with a prybar, or remove all screws.

How to Repair Small Holes in a Wall

Scrape or sand away any loose plaster, peeled paint, or wallboard face to ensure a solid base for patching.

Fill holes with lightweight spackle, using a putty knife.

Lightly sand the area with 150-grit sandpaper.

For a professional appearance, carefully check your walls for damage after a tear out, and repair the wallboard or plaster as needed. After a tearout it's almost inevitable that you'll need to patch holes in walls, especially small nail holes. But occasionally some of the wallboard face will come loose and that, too, needs to be repaired before attempting to install a new closet system. We recommend premixed patching compounds to reduce drying time. These quick-drying materials allow you to patch and paint a wall in the same day.

A. REMOVE LOOSE MATERIALS
Scrape, peel, or sand away any loose plaster, peeled paint, or wallboard face paper (tear off only loose paper, removing as little paper as possible) to ensure a solid base for patching.

B. FILL HOLES WITH SPACKLE
1. Fill holes with lightweight spackle. Apply the spackle with the smallest putty knife or wallboard knife that will span the entire hole.
2. Let the spackle dry.
   Note: For larger holes, you may need to apply two coats of spackle. Let the first coat dry completely before adding the second coat.

C. SAND & FINISH
1. Once the spackle is completely dry, sand the surface smooth with 150-grit sandpaper.
2. Wipe away dust with a slightly dampened sponge, and then prime the area with PVA primer.
3. Paint or finish the walls as desired before starting to design the interior for a new closet.

How to Repair a Large Wall Hole

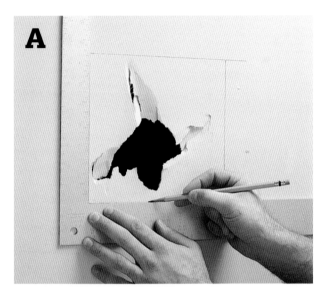

Outline the damaged area with a framing square. Cut away the damaged section with a jigsaw or drywall saw.

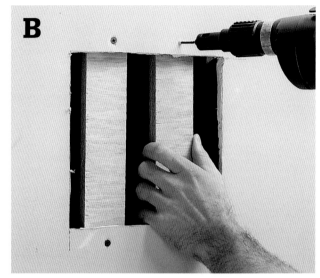

Install wood backer strips with 1¼" wallboard screws.

For large holes, it's best to replace that section of the wall instead of attempting to mend it. Here's how to patch a large hole in wallboard:

A. MEASURE THE DAMAGED AREA
1. Outline the damaged area with a framing square.
2. Use a wallboard saw or jigsaw to cut away the damaged section. *Note: Make sure there are no electrical wires or plumbing pipes in the wall before cutting.*

B. INSTALL BACKER STRIPS AND PATCH
1. Cut two pieces of wood to use as backer strips. Install the backer strips with 1¼" wallboard screws.
2. Cut a wallboard patch to size, and then screw the wallboard patch in place over the backer strips.
3. Cover the seams with self-adhesive mesh wallboard tape, and then apply wallboard compound. Let the compound dry completely, then add a second coat, and let it dry.

C. FINISHING TOUCHES
1. Use a slightly dampened sponge or wallboard wet-sander to smooth the repair area. This eliminates dust caused by dry sanding.
2. Sand the area smooth. Prime and repaint, if desired.

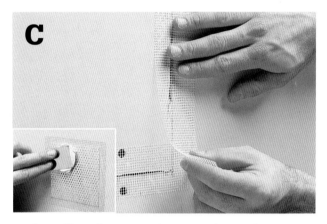

Apply wallboard tape over the seams, then apply two coats of wallboard compound and wet-sand the area (inset).

Tip ▶

If the hole is significant enough to patch but only a few inches in diameter, cover the entire hole with a peel-and-stick repair patch—backer strips and wallboard are not necessary in this scenario. The patch has a metal mesh center for strength and can be cut or shaped as needed. Use a wallboard knife to cover the patch with spackle or wallboard compound—two coats may be needed. Let the patch set until it is nearly dry and proceed to step C (this page).

How to Remove a Floor-based System

A. REMOVE ADJUSTABLE SHELVES & MOLDING

1. First remove all adjustable shelves and pins. Simply lift up on shelves and stack them outside of the closet. Pull stubborn pins out of verticals with pliers.
2. Moving across the entire length of the unit, wedge a prybar under the molding. Use a hammer to tap it in under the molding enough to loosen the molding from the unit. Once it is loosened, pry out the molding until you can completely remove it.
3. Remove tie or belt racks by wedging a slotted screwdriver behind the item and gently pushing away from the vertical. Once loose, pull the rack straight out, away from the vertical. *Note: If dowel screws were used, remove them with a screwdriver (check the dowel for a slotted or Phillips head).*

B. REMOVE ACCESSORIES & FIXED SHELVES

1. Completely remove all drawers, baskets, and other accessories; then remove the accompanying tracks from the verticals.
2. Disassemble the fixed shelves from the verticals. Starting at the top and at one end of the closet, unscrew all of the supporting screws or KDs and remove the top shelf. Repeat for each shelf in the section.
3. Unscrew the side-wall vertical from the wall.
4. Repeat the above steps for each section as you move along the wall. Set shelves and verticals outside of the closet.

C. FINISHING TOUCHES

1. Remove the floor support lumber. The lumber may have been nailed to the floor for extra stability—if so, gently pry up on the lumber until you can grip the nails with pliers and release them. Repeat for any ceiling supports. *Note: Such supports are most often used in built-in units, but they can be and occasionally are used in floor-based units.*
2. Using pliers and a wood strip to protect the floor, pull out any remaining nails for the floor. For extremely stubborn nails that are in the floor, use a nail set to sink them $\frac{1}{8}$" below the surface.
3. Fill the holes in the floor with wood putty. Fill the holes left in the wall with spackle. Allow the putty and spackle to completely dry.
4. Sand floor and wall patches smooth. Prime and paint the walls as desired.

Remove adjustable shelves by simply lifting them off pegs, then remove pegs. (Inset) Remove molding around the unit using a prybar.

Remove all accessories and their accompanying tracks. Also remove fixed shelves and their accompanying KD screws and dowels.

Use a pry bar to evenly pull up on floor supports that have been secured to the floor with nails. Once they are lifted, grab nails with pliers to remove them.

Adding Shelves

When considering shelves for your custom closet, choose materials appropriate for the loads they must support. Also keep in mind that because adjustable shelving does not provide support for the shelving unit, you can choose material more for design value than structural support. For example, a few tempered glass shelves for lighter loads add a decorative element unmatched by other materials.

The strength of a shelf depends on its material and the span—the distance between verticals or supports. In general, shelves should be no more than 36" long for clothing, shoes, and other lightweight storage (24" long if the shelving is made of tempered glass). For heavy items, such as books, shelf span must be shorter. Shelves longer than this will likely bow over time, and this places pressure on the verticals. The end result is often a closet system that caves in on itself. The days of caved-in closets are numbered thanks to modular systems. Modular closets incorporate verticals with brackets that fasten to wall rails. These wall rails make it virtually impossible for verticals to cave in, because each vertical is individually supported to the rail.

In contemporary closets, fixed shelves are often placed at the top, middle, and bottom of each section to add strength and support to the unit. Fixed shelves are placed wherever the added structural support is needed—for example, shelves on top and below a

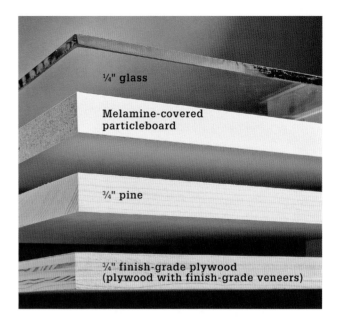

You can incorporate different shelving materials in your custom design. The most common shelving materials are shown here (above) and are shown in order of strength.

row of drawers will be fixed to add structural support to this heavier area. Fixed shelves are fastened to the verticals and at the same time joined together through the verticals with modular hardware or basic joinery methods (see next page), thus they are able to share weight and add overall strength to the entire closet unit. Fixed shelves also are screwed to the wall (either with cleats or L-brackets). Other shelves are adjustable, set on metal brackets or pins that are fit into holes in verticals.

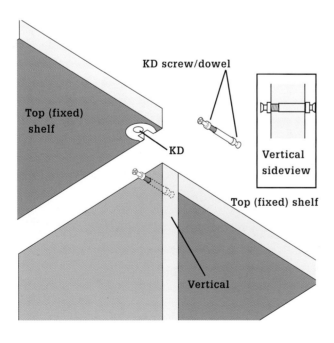

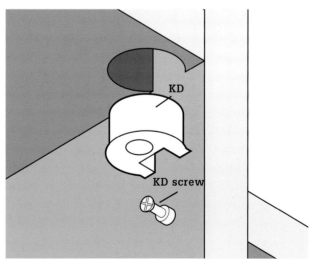

Knock-down fittings (KDs) hold the top shelf in place but also support the adjoining shelves on opposite sides of each adjacent vertical. This creates a solid, cohesive, and sturdy unit.

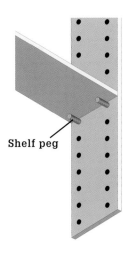

Shelf peg

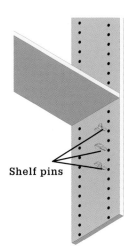

Shelf pins

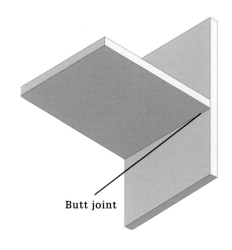

Butt joint

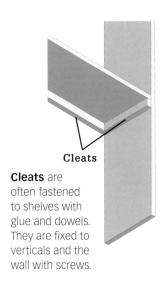

Cleats

Cleats are often fastened to shelves with glue and dowels. They are fixed to verticals and the wall with screws.

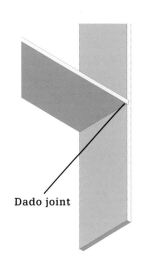

Dado joint

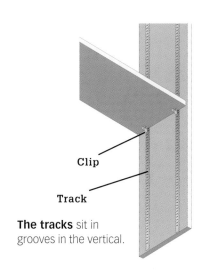

Clip

Track

The tracks sit in grooves in the vertical.

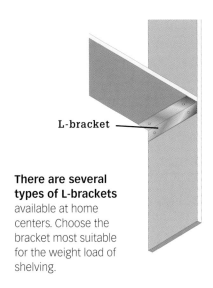

L-bracket

There are several types of L-brackets available at home centers. Choose the bracket most suitable for the weight load of shelving.

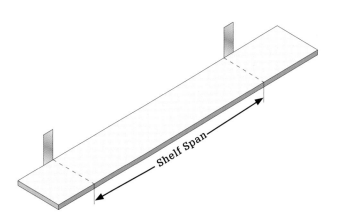

Shelf Span

Shelf span is the distance between verticals. A shorter span strengthens a shelf.

Modular Shelves

Modular shelves are constructed with standardized dimensions, allowing flexibility and variety in use. These modular shelves hold together wall-hung or floor-based units. The KDs used in the shelves allow each shelf to lock into the supporting vertical and the adjacent shelf on the other side of the vertical. The depth of verticals is determined in the design stage. Standard depths range from 12 to 18".

How to Prepare Modular Shelves

Tools & Materials ▸

¾" melamine sheet or shelf stock	Measuring tape
Circular saw with melamine blade	Pegboard scrap
	Clamps
Planer	KDs
Drill with ¼" bit	Phillips screwdriver
20 mm bit (or size recommended by KD manufacturer)	Heat-activated veneer tape
	Iron
	Scraper
Right-angle drill guide	Hardwood block
	Cloth

A. CUT VERTICALS

1. Measure and mark cutlines for each vertical panel.
2. Cut verticals to size using a circular saw with a melamine blade. Shelving stock makes for a good straightedge; be sure to allow for cut waste from the blade (or at least ⅛").
3. Smooth rough edges down to the exact cutline with a planer. *Note: If your circular saw is cutting smoothly, this step is not necessary.*

B. MARK & DRILL PIN HOLES ON VERTICALS

1. Mount a drill and ¼" bit in a right-angle drill guide. Set the drill-stop for ⅜" depth. Mark the centers of first two pin holes ⅜" down from the top edges of the verticals and approximately 1½" in from side edges. *Note: The placement of two rows of shelf-pin holes from edges may slightly vary; the key is to be consistent (all factory or store-purchased stock materials with predrilled holes work for projects in this book).*
2. On the inside face of one of the verticals, align the factory edge of a pegboard scrap flush with the vertical edge. Align a hole in the pegboard over the ⅜" marks. Clamp the pegboard in place. Repeat step 3 to drill pin holes on inside face of remaining vertical(s).
3. Drill two rows of parallel holes in each riser, about 1½" from the edges of the riser, using the pegboard as a guide. *Note: These holes also provide the placement points for KDs. Follow specific instructions for pin-hole alignment from the manufacturer of the hardware you use.*

C. CUT ADJUSTABLE SHELVES

1. Measure the width between verticals (which is determined by your custom design) and cut shelves to size. For modular units, build shelves to be flush with the front edges of verticals (in other words, the same depth as verticals).
2. Make a jig by cutting a 6"-wide × 16"-long (or at least 2" wider than your cut material) piece of melamine shelving stock. Use this as a cutting guide. Clamp the factory edge of your guide to the appropriate distance from the cutline (allowing for your saw's base and blade size).
3. Cut your shelves to size using a circular saw with a melamine blade.

D. PREPARE FIXED SHELVES

1. Cut shelves to size following step C above.
2. Align the top of the fixed shelf flush with tops of verticals.
3. Mark KD locations on underside of shelf on center to predrilled holes in vertical.
4. Predrill holes for KDs according to manufacturer instructions at marked locations on underside of shelf.
5. Press KDs into drilled holes on underside of shelf to check for an accurate fit.

E. FINISHING TOUCHES

1. Use heat-activated veneer tape to cover unfinished edges that are seen. Bond the tape with a household iron (or edgebander).
2. Rub the tape with a block of hardwood covered in cloth for a smooth finish. Trim ends and edges with a scraper.

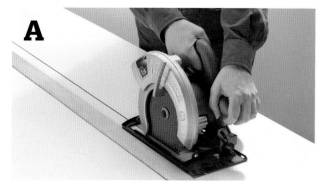

Mark cutlines for verticals and allow for (at least) ⅛" waste. Cut verticals with a circular saw with a melamine blade. Smooth edges down to actual cutlines with a planer.

Measure ⅜" on center to first shelf-pin hole down from the top cut edge of vertical. Align pegboard holes to first two marks and about 1½" from side edges of vertical. Drill two rows of parallel holes in each vertical, using the pegboard as a guide.

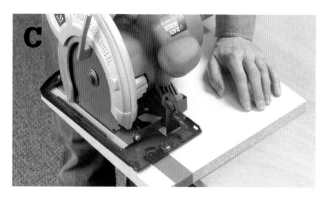

Cut the shelves according to your custom design, using a circular saw with a melamine blade.

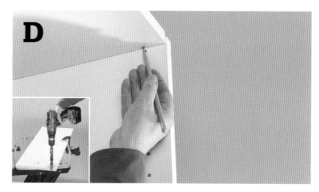

Mark KD locations on top fixed shelf, and then (inset) drill holes for KDs. Repeat for all fixed shelves.

Apply heat-activated veneer tape to all exposed edges for a finished appearance.

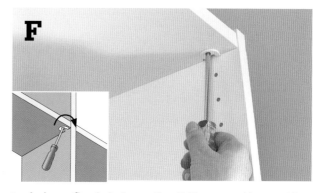

Lock down fixed shelves with a Phillips screwdriver. Position the screwdriver at 25° and twist clockwise until top shelf and vertical are pulled together.

F. INSTALLING FIXED SHELVES

1. Drill KD screws into the predrilled holes on verticals. Lower the top shelf into place.
2. Lock down shelf KDs over KD screws using a screwdriver.
3. Repeat this process for each fixed shelf.

Note: For fixed shelves that align with another fixed shelf on the other side of the same vertical, use a KD screw and dowel or ("connector bolt").

4. Plumb and level the entire unit; then fasten each fixed shelf to the wall with two steel L-brackets.

Metal Standards

Metal standards fit into grooves on verticals, offering a neat, flush finished look. They are inexpensive and effective for medium to heavy loads so long as the shelf span is 16" or less and ¾"-thick, finish-grade plywood is used (or similar sturdy material).

Tools & Materials ▸

Marking gauge
Router and straight
   bit
Hacksaw
Shelf standards and
   hardware

Heat-activated veneer
   tape
Iron
Hardwood block
Utility knife
Sandpaper

Mark two parallel dado grooves on the inside face of each vertical. Insert metal standards to check for an accurate fit, and then cut the standards to size.

How to Install Metal Standards

A. PREPARE VERTICALS

1. Mark two parallel dado grooves on the inside face of each vertical using a marking gauge. Grooves should be at least 1" from the edges.
2. Cut dadoes to depth and thickness of metal standards using a router. Test-fit standards to make sure they fit, and then remove them.

B. FASTEN STANDARDS TO VERTICALS

Cut metal standards to fit into dadoes. Make sure slots are aligned so shelves are level, then fasten standards with manufacturer nails or screws.

Attach the metal standards using nails or screws provided by the manufacturer.

C. FINISHING TOUCHES

1. Build shelves to fit in between verticals (measure the exact distance between verticals), then insert shelf clips into the slots on the metal standards. Install the shelves.
2. Finish shelves with heat-activated veneer tape. Bond the tape. Bond the tape with a household iron, then rub the tape with a block of hardwood. Trim the edges with utility knife.

Insert shelf clips into the slots on the metal standards for adjustable shelves.

Fixed Shelves

Contrary to cabinetry, most closet systems do not have a solid sheet of backing along the unit. It is not necessary to have the backing piece because fixed shelves and wall rails (which support each vertical) provide the structural support needed. Closet systems "fix" top, middle, and bottom shelves (see page 44).

Units supported by nailers (instead of a rail with adjustable features) require fixed shelves with wood or melamine cleats, because it is the cleat that ultimately holds the entire unit to the wall (not the verticals). Fasten wood cleats to top, middle, and bottom shelves—the nailer stabilizes the verticals before you fasten the fixed shelves to the wall.

How to Prepare Fixed Shelves with Cleats

A. DRILL DOWEL HOLES

1. Measure and cut shelves to size, using a circular saw with a melamine blade.
2. Align the precut shelf with the cleat (which is cut 2" shorter in length) as they will look when the joint is finished: center the cleat on the underside of shelf, flush with the backside. Mark for dowel holes every 3 to 4" on the shelf and cleat.
3. Drill dowel holes in the shelf at $^1/_2$" deep, and holes in the cleat at $1^1/_4$" deep.

B. FASTEN CLEAT TO SHELF

1. Test-fit the pieces by inserting $1^1/_2$" fluted dowels in the cleat and tapping the shelf in place. Deepen the dowel holes as needed.
2. Separate pieces and remove dowels, then apply glue (appropriate for your shelving and cleat material) to the dowels and insert them into the holes in the shelf. Also apply glue to the flat surfaces being joined. *Note: When joining melamine, apply glue to dowels only (not the flat surfaces).*

C. FINISH

Assemble pieces, tapping them with a wood mallet until the joint is snug. Completely wipe away any excess glue, using a damp cloth. Allow the glue to completely dry.

Tools & Materials ▶

Circular saw with melamine blade	Iron
Drill	Hardwood block
$1^1/_2$" fluted wood dowels	Utility knife or scraper
Wood mallet	1 × 2 cleats
Glue	¾"-thick melamine shelf stock without predrilled holes
Heat-activated veneer tape	

Drill ½"-deep dowel holes every 3" to 4" on the shelves, and drill 1¼"-deep dowel holes every 3" to 4" on the cleats.

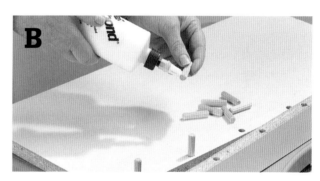

Apply glue to the dowels and insert them into the shelf holes. Fasten the 1×2 cleat to shelf with 1½" fluted dowels in the cleat.

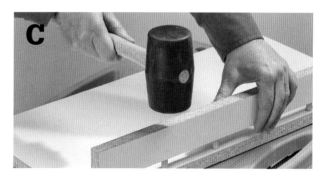

Tap the cleat and shelf together with a rubber mallet, and allow to dry.

Installing Corner Units

There are two or three good techniques for getting the most out of your corner spaces. The one you ultimately choose will depend on your needs and complete design. To incorporate these corner projects into your custom designs or other projects in this book, you want to start here—with planning and understanding how to deal with the corners in your closet. Once you have your corner designs chosen, then you can plan the rest of your closet.

The first option is to have your back wall unit fit flush into the corner while the perpendicular side unit ends at least 12" away from the corner. This allows you to get maximum use out of the back wall space and still leaves ample room to walk behind the side unit to reach clothing stored in the corner. You could also make the walking space large enough to tuck a bench behind the side unit for a private dressing area. Another option is to leave the space on the back wall (instead of the side wall) open with a space of at least 12". Which wall you choose to leave open is largely dependent on maximizing storage (see design example on page 34).

If your closet unit's top shelf is well above your head, you can choose the first option (above) but add a top connecting shelf between the back and side wall units. This gives a more finished, modular appearance and provides extra storage space on the top shelf. You could take this a step further and add custom cabinets all along the top shelf.

If you prefer all of your items to be visible from the center of the closet, you can build special corner unit shelves. These corner units are the same depth as the side units to ensure a streamline flow around the entire closet. They can be wall-hung or floor-based units. If you prefer to hang clothes in the corner, you can leave out the shelves and add closet rods. The rod runs along either the back or side wall, so that one end is attached directly to the wall.

Yet another method is to fit end corners flush together and place a supporting spacer behind. This is a common method used in cabinetry. It provides a nice, finished look but it doesn't allow you to use the triangular space in the corner. It is appropriate for built-ins—in this situation the triangular space behind is not necessary, for the built-in extends to the ceiling (thus making up for any lost storage space in the corner).

The final consideration is outside corners. This gives a finished look to side- or back-wall units that are not flush against a wall. There are many applications for this in a walk-in closet. You may want to reserve a corner of the closet for a vanity or bench, for example. But instead of the end unit on either side of that area being unfinished you can have extra shelving.

Connector Top Shelf

For this project, the wall units are hung and then a top shelf joins the side and back units for a finished top shelf around the entire closet. A standard application is to use the entire back wall for storage (in other words, the shelving butts up to each side wall) while leaving the sides just short of the back wall—by a minimum of 12". This leaves ample room to access the items stored on the back wall shelf right into the corner, so long as the top shelf is tall enough for you to stand under the joining shelf.

For ease of explanation, this project will assume that certain standards are in place for the existing back- and side-wall units: The standard distance in between the side and back wall units (length) is 12", minimum. The standard depth for shelving is 14". The standard thickness of modular shelving material is ¾".

Tools, Materials & Cutting List ▸

Circular saw with melamine blade
Screwdriver
Drill
Iron (optional)
Measuring tape
Rubber mallet

¾ × 12 × 24" melamine sheet
Painter's tape
Heat-activated veneer tape (optional)
Connector brackets (or H-channels)
⅝" panhead screws
Knock-down (KDs) fasteners
KD screws and dowels

Key	Part	Dimension	Pcs.	Material
A	Corner Shelf*	12 × 14 × ¾"	1	¾"-thick melamine

* Cut to fit.

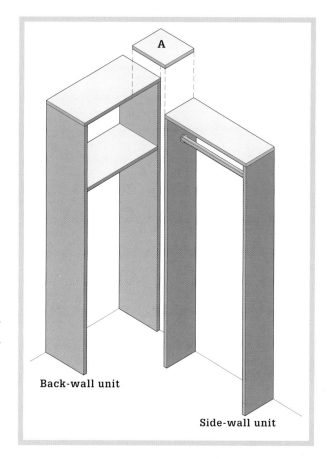

Back-wall unit

Side-wall unit

How to Join Units in Corners

A. MEASURING THE CORNER

1. After your entire closet design is completed and the wall units are in place (whether wall-hung or floor-based), measure the distance in between the back-wall unit and side-wall unit at the top of the two units, where the top shelf insert will rest. Then measure the depth of the side wall unit.
2. Make sure all four contact points are square. If they are not, adjust your wall units until they are square.

B. MARK CUTLINES

Using a pencil, mark your measurements in a corner of the melamine sheet. If the space was square, it should be 12 × 14". Make sure the corner of the melamine sheet is square to the wall as well. *Note: If the wall is angled, transfer this angle to the piece you are about to cut. Determine the angle by using an angle finder. Alternative: Purchase shelf stock of the appropriate depth and simply cut to length.*

C. CUT THE TOP SHELF

1. Using painter's tape, place tape along the outside edges of your marks. This helps to prevent chipping when cutting a slight angle.

2. Using a sharp circular saw with a melamine blade, cut out the top shelf following your premarked lines.
3. Remove the painter's tape.
4. Finish the outside (front) edge with heat-activated veneer tape (see page 47).

D. ATTACH THE TOP SHELF

1. If KD screws were used on the side-wall vertical, remove them and replace with screws and dowels. Insert a KD screw through one side of a shelf-pin hole in the vertical and a dowel through the other side of the vertical. *Note: This strengthens the unit by fastening the two top shelves together through the vertical, distributing weight between the two sections.*
2. Hold the top shelf in place and mark the KD locations on the bottom of the top shelf. They should be on center to the predrilled shelf-pin holes on the vertical.
3. Drill a hole on the underside edge of the top shelf at your marks for a KD (see page 47).
4. Press the KDs into the predrilled holes. Place the shelf down on top of the KD screws. All sides should be flush with the back- and side-wall units. Lock down the KDs by tightening the KD onto the screw with a screwdriver. *Note: If the shelf is not flush, check the screw fitting into the KD to determine the cause. You may get by with redrilling a KD hole and filling in the extra space from the*

Measure the space in between the back and side units, using an angle finder for wall sides that are not square.

Transfer your measurements to a sheet of melamine (or shelf stock without predrilled holes).

Cut the top shelf, using a circular saw with a melamine blade. Place painter's tape along cut lines to prevent chipping—this is especially helpful for cutting angles.

old hole with strong glue. Once the glue dries, fit the shelf in place again. If this repair seems to jeopardize the strength of the unit, cut a new shelf piece and better align the predrilled KD holes.

5. Lower the top shelf into place over the screws. Attach the connector bracket by driving $\frac{5}{8}$" screws into the predrilled locations.

6. Using a screwdriver, lock down the KDs. This will in turn pull down the top shelf into place and pull together the top shelf insert and side wall unit vertical.

7. Once the KDs are tightened, the top piece should be flush with the top of the side- and back-wall units. The front of the top shelf will be flush with the fronts of the unit as well. Align the pieces so all sides are flush and level.

E. MARK THE CONNECTOR BRACKET LOCATION

1. With the top shelf in place (with the KDs locked down), measure away from the side wall 4" and make a mark on the top shelf (on the side butted up against the back-wall unit). From that mark, measure in another 4" away from the side wall and make another mark on the top shelf.

2. Align the connector bracket screw holes over the marks and centered over the top shelf and back-wall unit (the minimum suggested length for the bracket is 2").

3. Make a mark where the other connector bracket screw holes are on the back wall unit. Set the top shelf on the floor.

4. Remove top shelf.

F. FASTEN THE CONNECTOR BRACKET

1. Predrill holes from the top down at your 4" marks on the back wall unit for $\frac{5}{8}$" screws.

2. Predrill holes from the top down at your 4" marks on the top shelf for $\frac{5}{8}$" screws.

3. Reattach the top shelf by following the directions in step E, making sure the finished edge faces forward.

4. Fasten the brackets to the top shelf and back-wall unit with panhead screws drilled into predrilled holes.

Tip ▸

If the unit is square and you're using a short length of melamine to cut the corner piece, you can predrill the KD holes on one side of the shelf. Align the shelf against the back-wall shelf and the side-wall vertical; then simply trace a line on the underside of the shelf for the cutline.

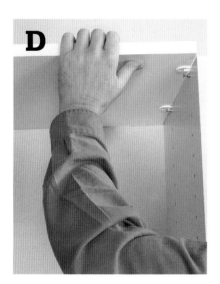

D

Remove the existing screw in the end vertical and insert a screw that fits a dowel. Lower the shelf back down into place over the screw and lock down KDs.

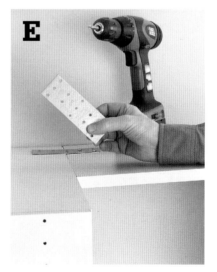

E

Mark the screw hole placement for the connector brackets. Most flat brackets or H-channels like the one shown will work. Simply use two panhead screws on either side to fasten to the back-wall top shelf and connector shelf.

F

Fasten the brackets to the back-wall top shelf and the connecting shelf with panhead screws.

Corner Shelf Units

A corner shelf unit can be wall-hung or floor-based (the same basic procedures and templates are needed). For a floor-based unit you essentially create a corner cabinet (with or without doors), making sure the corner unit and adjoining wall units are plumb. This unit is most sturdy with a thin plywood backing. There are a few extra steps for a modular wall-hung unit (which does not have backing), so we will explain that in detail now. Install the corner-shelving unit before installing the units on the adjacent walls, if possible.

You must first determine how far you want the corner unit to extend along each wall. Standard

corner shelves for modular units range from 24 to 34" long. The standard minimum height is 12" up from the floor, but we will say 20" for this project—this provides enough storage space under the shelves for boots. Finally, you must determine the overall height of the verticals. This project is 60" tall. This ensures ample room for 5 corner shelves, double-hanging rods, or a single rod for long-hang space. These are dimensions you'll want to customize for your closet. *Note:* For floor-based units, check for significant differences in floor height ($^5/_{16}$" or more) and plan to cut verticals accordingly (or use shims).

Tools

Drill
Screwdriver
Rubber mallet
Circular saw with melamine blade
Jigsaw with melamine blade
Hacksaw
Ruler
Router
Hammer
Iron
Graph paper
Level
Measuring tape
Stud finder
Cardboard ruler
Compass

Materials

(1) $\frac{3}{4}$" × 4 × 8' melamine sheet to cut out corner
   shelves (see template)
(1) $\frac{3}{4}$" × 4 × 8' melamine sheet or precut verticals
   14" wide × 60" long
Hanging rail
Knock-down (KD) fasteners
KD screws and dowels
$2\frac{1}{2}$" drywall screws
Toggle bolts to fit $2\frac{1}{2}$" machine screws
Self-drilling wall anchors with $1\frac{1}{4}$" screws
8d finish nails
2" drywall screws
20 mm bit (or bit size recommended by KD
   manufacturer)
Heat-activated veneer tape
$\frac{3}{4}$" panhead screws
Euro, barrel, or $\frac{5}{8}$" panhead screws
2" wood screws
1 × 3 melamine cleat material

Cutting List

Corner shelves (3, plus adjustable shelves as desired):

Key	Part	Dimension	Pcs.	Material
A	Corner shelves	$\frac{3}{4}$"-thick, 14 × 24"	3	melamine
B	Verticals	$\frac{3}{4}$ × 14 × 60"	3	melamine
C	Rods	24" long	(1 or 2, as desired)*	metal
D	Wall rail	48" long		
E	Wall rail	15" long		

* Alternative option to adding adjustable shelves; measure final
space for accurate fit.

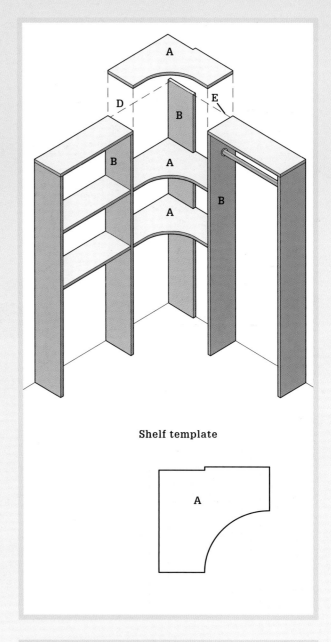

Shelf template

A

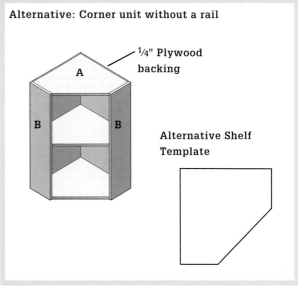

Alternative: Corner unit without a rail

$\frac{1}{4}$" Plywood backing

Alternative Shelf Template

How to Make a Corner Unit for a Wall-hung System

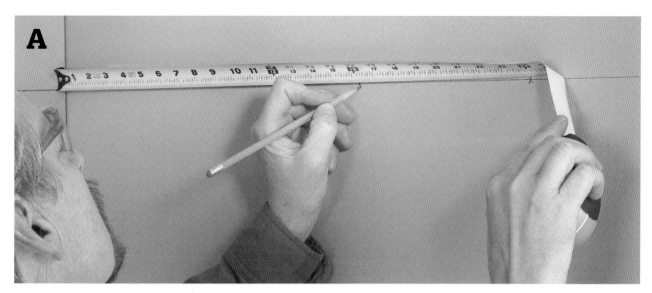

Draw a level line at 80" up from the floor (the height of the closet unit). Then make an X along the line drawn on this wall at 14 and 24" from the corner.

A. DETERMINE THE RAIL PLACEMENT

1. Graph out your closet on a piece of graph paper.
2. To mark the wall where you want the bottom of the verticals to hang, measure from the floor up to 20" and make a mark on the wall. Draw a level line across the wall at this height. *Note: For floor-based units set a level on the floor along various locations around the perimeter of your closet to determine if your floor is level. Note any significant differences in floor height on the graph paper.*
3. Measure up 60" from the side-wall line you just made (at 20" up from the floor) and draw another level line.
4. Hold a tape measure in the corner near the floor and measure 24" out from that corner along the 20" height marks on the side wall (at top level line). Make an X where the 20 and 24" marks intersect. Repeat for the back wall.
5. Measure from the corner out 14" on the side wall (for the vertical to be placed in the notched section) and make another X.

Note: Make sure your marks are all level to each other. If your floor slightly slants down along one wall, your marks on both walls must remain level to each other. It is quite common for walls and floors to not be perfectly straight, but if you have significant structural problems, stop now and contact your local building inspector before continuing with your project.

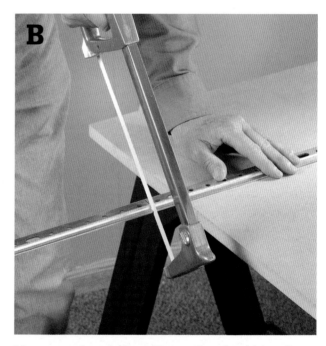

Measure and mark the cutline on the rail. Hold the rail steady on a table and cut with a hacksaw.

B. MEASURE AND CUT RAIL TO SIZE

1. Use a stud finder to locate and mark studs on wall.
2. Using a hacksaw, cut the back-wall rail to 48" long (or at least twice the length of your custom corner shelf length). Cut the side-wall rail to 15" long.

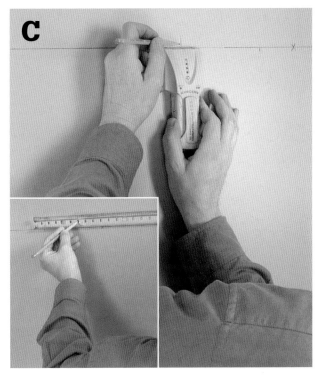

Mark stud locations on the wall using a stud finder. (Inset) Hold the rail on wall to mark screw locations, and then predrill holes at studs.

C. INSTALL RAILS ON WALL

1. Align the track right into the corner on the back wall. Depending on the type of rail brackets/ hangers you are using, align the track so that once the verticals are hanging on the tracks the vertical tops will be flush with your height marks.

2. Hold rail in place along back wall. Check for level. Adjust as necessary until level. Mark screw locations according to track manufacturer's specifications.

3. Predrill $\frac{1}{2}$" pilot holes at the marked locations that hit a stud.

4. Hold the rail in place again. Wherever you cannot hit a stud, use toggle bolts; otherwise, attach the track with $2\frac{1}{2}$" drywall screws drilled through pilot holes.

5. Install the side-wall track (notched shelf side) in the same manner. Stop this track at least 15" from the corner. Determine exact placement by measuring out 15" and then locating the nearest stud. Adjust the placement of this track so that screws hit studs where possible—especially at the end point closest to the corner.

6. Slide the track cover over the track for a finished appearance.

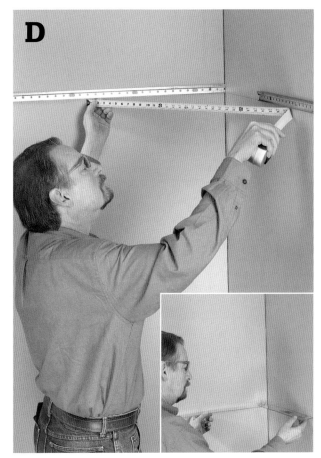

Check the corner for square using the 3-4-5 method. If the corner is obviously not square, use an angle finder in the corner out 24".

D. CHECK CORNER FOR SQUARE

To check for square in the corner, mark a spot 3 ft. from the corner on the side wall; then, mark a spot 4 ft. from the corner on the back wall. Measure between the marks. If the distance between the marks is exactly 5 ft., the walls are square. It is common to allow $\frac{1}{2}$" ($\frac{1}{4}$" on either side of the corner) to be off square. A slight deviation of $\frac{1}{2}$" total or less from 90° will not affect the installation procedure. *Note: If the corner is not square or intentionally curved, use an angle finder to determine the corner angles.*

To notch a section in the corner for a vertical support, first measure the depth of the vertical panels (usually 14"). Starting in the corner of your template, measure this distance out along the side wall. This is where a supporting corner vertical panel will be placed. Measure in from this line the same thickness of the vertical panel (usually $\frac{3}{4}$"). This section needs to be cut out to fit around the vertical panel. See the Corner Shelf illustration on page 55.

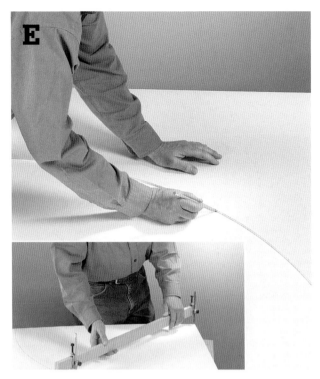

Create a cutting template for accurate measurements. Use this guide for each cut piece to follow. (Inset) Use a compass to create a slight arch from the two depth endpoints. This is the front of the shelf.

E. CREATE A CUTTING TEMPLATE

1. Transfer your measurements from step D onto a scrap of melamine that you can use as a template for cutting the shelves. Do this for both the back and side walls.
2. Determine the depth of your wall units (this is most often 14"). Take that amount and transfer it to your template for the two sides that will adjoin to the other wall units. They should be 90° to the back- and side-wall lines (refer to the shelf template on page 55).
3. For a straight front edge, simply use a ruler to connect the two endpoints. *Tip: Use a compass to create a slight arch from the two depth endpoints. This is the front of the shelf.*
4. Cut out the template with a circular saw. Save the curve for last and cut that one with a jigsaw.
5. Place your template in the corner to see how accurate your measurements are and how well it fits. If you discover that room corners are not square or that walls are uneven by more than $\frac{1}{2}$" ($\frac{1}{4}$" on either side of the corner), you will need to purchase trim pieces—base shoe or cove moldings or wall shims—to cover gaps between the walls and your corner unit. Measure these gaps now to make purchasing the shims later easier.

After tracing around the cutting template, cut out the shelf. Use a jigsaw for the curve.

F. CUT THE SHELVES

1. Using a circular saw, cut out your corner top piece using the template as a guide. Cut along all the marks except the curve, save that for last.
2. Once your top piece is cut out, rough-cut along the curve with the jigsaw, leaving a $\frac{1}{8}$" space in between the cutline and the jigsaw.
3. Use a router to remove the remaining $\frac{1}{8}$" along the cutline. *Note: This ensures a smooth, finished cutline that is otherwise difficult to achieve with a jigsaw, making it easier to apply edgebanding later. Melamine edges are often drilled or power planed instead of sanded because it is difficult to sand a smooth edge on melamine.*
4. Cut out the notched section using the jigsaw.
5. Repeat this process for the middle and bottom shelf. The bottom shelf for a wall-hung unit will most likely be at least 12" up from the floor (20" for this project).
6. Finish exposed edges that you will see from inside the closet with heat-activated veneer tape (see page 47).

Fasten rail brackets to verticals with ¾" panhead screws.

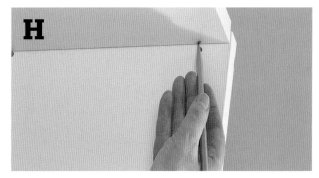

Mark six KD locations on the underside of each top shelf.

G. CUT VERTICALS AND INSTALL BRACKETS

1. Using a circular saw, cut three verticals from ¾"-thick melamine shelving stock with predrilled holes each 60" long and 14" wide.
2. Cut out a notch on the verticals to allow them to fit over the wall rail and still be flush to the wall.
3. Fasten the rail brackets to the verticals according to manufacturer instructions, using ¾" panhead screws.
4. Hang the two end verticals on their respective rails, 24⅜" from the corner. Use a level to make sure they are all level to each other. *Note: The distance from the corner in which you hang verticals is dependent on the length of the corner shelves plus the thickness of the vertical. If your shelf is 30" from the corner, hang the shelves 30¾" from the corner.*

H. MARK KD LOCATIONS ON FIXED SHELVES

Align the top shelf with a vertical. On the underside of the top shelf, mark the KD hole locations on center to shelf-pin holes on verticals. Repeat for all six-KD locations in order to attach the shelf to the side-wall, back-wall, and corner verticals (see page 55).

I. PREDRILL KD LOCATIONS ON FIXED SHELVES

1. Predrill the four holes for the KDs on the bottom edge of the top shelf, using a 20mm bit (or bit size recommended by KD manufacturer).
2. Repeat for the middle and bottom shelves.
3. Insert two KD dowels into the predrilled holes on one side of an end vertical, leaving them stick out slightly in order to lower the KD in the shelf over them. *Note: Eventually, this will allow you to fit two KD screws into the other side of the vertical to allow for top shelves on both sides of the end vertical.*
4. Repeat this process for the other end vertical.
5. Insert KD screws only on the inner (notched) vertical.

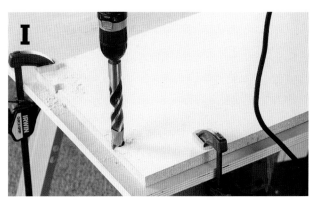

Predrill holes for KDs following manufacturer recommendations.

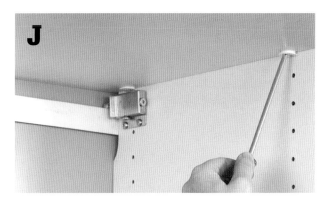

Lower the top corner shelf in place and lock down KD screw/dowels on either corner side.

J. ATTACH FIXED CORNER SHELVES

1. Make sure all KD screws and dowels fit together through the verticals. Tap the KDs into the predrilled holes on the underside of the fixed shelf, using a rubber mallet if needed. Lower the shelf into place, fitting KDs over screws.
2. Using a screwdriver, lock down the KDs on the top shelf to the notched vertical panel.
3. Repeat this entire process for the middle and then bottom shelves.

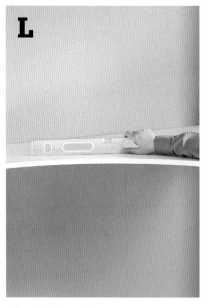

Fasten L-bracket supports to the wall with 2" stud screws (or if you cannot hit a stud, use hollow wall anchors and screws). Fasten the L-bracket to the underside of the vertical with ¾" panhead screws.

Check for level on the fixed shelves. Also check the verticals for plumb. Make adjustments as necessary before moving on.

Alternative: Install a closet rod instead of shelving at desired heights. Fasten to wall with a 2" stud screw or drywall screws driven into anchors. Fasten to closet vertical with Euro or barrel screws.

K. ADD SUPPORTS TO VERTICALS

Attach L-bracket supports to the wall and the underside of verticals 20" above the floor, using 2" wood screws driven into studs and panhead screws driven up into verticals. Where you cannot hit a stud, predrill holes for wall anchors and then fasten the screw through the anchor into the wall. *Note: The verticals rest right on top of the supports. Most closet installers will purchase L-brackets that are small enough to be concealed under the vertical (in other words, no wider than ¾").*

L. LEVEL AND PLUMB THE UNIT

1. Before moving on it is important to make sure the entire unit is plumb and level. Adjust rail brackets for plumb, if necessary. For unlevel shelves, unlock KDs and realign fixed shelves.
2. If this doesn't settle the shelf, attempt to place some pressure on the shelf to get it to sit level.
3. If this still doesn't work, carefully check each KD to make sure they are all sitting flush with the underside of the shelf. Tap any loose KDs into the predrilled holes with a rubber mallet.
4. Measure from the top down to the center of the holes that have KD screws or dowels in them. All vertical holes must be level to each other.

5. As a last resort, you may need to cut a new shelf and predrill the KD holes again to make sure they fit on center with vertical holes.
6. Now that your entire structure is solid and each piece is flush with other adjoining pieces, you may want to take the time to add adjustable shelving. Fasten shelf pins to verticals at predrilled-hole locations. Simply slide the shelving into place on top of the pins.

ALTERNATIVE

If you'd prefer to install closet rods, measure down from the top of the top shelf so that the rod will be placed just beneath the rail on the back wall (the wall without the notch). The rod will be on the same side as the notched vertical. This allows you to have one side screwed directly into the wall for added stability.

1. Using 2" drywall screws (or wall anchors and screws specified by the manufacturer) drill the first rod end directly into the back wall.
2. Install the other rod end into the vertical panel, using Euro or barrel screws. If these screws are difficult to find, you can also use ⅝" panhead screws.
3. Follow the manufacturer's directions to place the closet rod.

Alternative: How to Make a Corner Unit without a Wall Rail

Tools & Materials ▸

Level	1¼" panhead screws
Stud finder	1 × 2 cleat material
Measuring tape	8d finish nails
Cardboard template	¾" × 13¾ × 34"
Circular saw with	verticals
melamine blade	¾" × 14 × 24" corner
Jigsaw with	shelves
melamine blade	¼" × 13½" × 24"
Drill	plywood backing
2½" drywall screws	White paint

A. PREPARE NAILER

1. Use a studfinder to locate studs on the wall.
2. Mark level lines at 17 and 80" up from the floor.
3. Cut two bottom nailers out of 1 × 4, ¾"-thick plywood. Fasten them to the wall with 2½" drywall screws at studs along line at 17".

B. PREPARE CORNER UNIT

1. Create a template and cut the middle, top, and bottom fixed shelves for the first box.
2. Install 1 × 3 shelf sleats on center along back- and side-wall edges of each fixed shelf.

3. Cut three verticals pieces to 10⁵⁄₁₆", using a circular saw.
4. Set the shelf on top of the vertical. Drive a screw through the vertical side and into the shelf. Repeat for the other two verticals.
5. Repeat step 4 for the middle and bottom shelves. Fasten the bottom shelf flush to the bottom of the vertical.
6. Measure and cut ¼" plywood back panel to fit flush with the wall-side edges of the corner unit. Position the panels with the grain running vertically. Attach them along the entire perimeter of the corner unit with ¾" panhead screws every 4 or 5".

C. INSTALL CORNER UNIT

1. Set your box directly on top of the nailer and have a helper check for level and plumb; then drill pilot holes through the cleats and into the wall. Set the unit down and determine which holes hit studs and which ones do not—those that will not hit a stud, drill a hole for a toggle bolt.
2. Align the box again and fasten it to the wall, using drywall screws at studs and toggle bolts in drywall.
3. Stagger three more 1¼" panhead screws by drilling through the top of the bottom shelf down into the supporting nailer.
4. Repeat the above steps, stacking two more box units on top of the existing one.

Fasten 1 × 4 nailers to the wall with 2½" drywall screws at studs.

Secure panels to the perimeter of the corner unit with ¾" panhead screws.

Rest the unit on the nailer and then fasten drywall screws at the top inside and outside corners.

Outside Corner Units

A nice finished look for wall units that stop short of the corner is an outside corner unit. This basic design can be used for a floor-based or wall-hung unit.

How to Make an Outside Corner Unit

A. PREPARE VERTICALS

1. Cut two verticals to sit flush with the top shelves of the wall-hung unit while they extend to the floor.
2. Drill holes for adjustable shelves along both sides of each vertical (see page 46). Be sure to measure down from the top edge ⅜" and make a mark. This is the (on center) placement for the first shelf-pin holes, and then align the first pin-hole to those marks. *Alternative: Purchase shelf stock at the desired depth with predrilled pinholes, and cut to the desired height.*
3. Remove the existing end vertical if it is wall-hung, and replace it with the new end vertical cut in step 1 (above) that extends to the floor.
4. Place the second "wall" vertical along the wall and flush up against the end vertical, so the two are square in the corner, and check that the two new verticals are level along the top.

B. INSTALL VERTICALS

1. Secure the vertical to the wall with two 1½" drywall screws along the top of the vertical and two 1½" drywall screws along the bottom of the vertical, centered inside the shelf-pin holes and approximately ¼" from ends.
2. Use 1¼" panhead screws through the inside of the end vertical and into the edge of the wall vertical.

C. PREPARE AND INSTALL SHELVES

1. Make a template for the shelves on cardboard. Cut the plywood out to serve as a cutting guide.
2. Cut the top, middle, and bottom shelves using a circular saw for the straight sides and a jigsaw for the front curve.
3. Mark the shelves for KD screw holes on center to predrilled shelf-pin holes on end and wall verticals.

Measure from the top of the existing wall-hung unit to the floor. Cut two new verticals (at same depth as existing unit) to this height.

4. Drill the four KD holes on the underside of each shelf (see page 46). Insert KDs into the holes, tapping them in with a rubber mallet if necessary.
5. Insert KD screw/dowels on the end vertical and screw on the wall vertical. Lower the shelf down into place, fitting KDs over screw/dowels. Lock down the top shelf using a Phillips screwdriver. Repeat for the middle and then bottom shelves.
6. Check the verticals for plumb, and adjust rail brackets as necessary, following the manufacturer instructions.
7. Fill in extra adjustable shelves as desired, using shelf pins in the predrilled holes on the vertical.

Fasten the two verticals together with 1½" screws. Work from the interior of the existing unit and drill the screw into the end of the wall vertical.

Install adjustable shelves on shelf pins. Fixed shelves (at top, middle, and bottom) are fastened to the existing unit with KD screw/dowels (KD screws on the new corner vertical).

Tools, Materials & Cutting List ▸

Measuring tape
Circular saw with
   melamine blade
Jigsaw with melamine
   blade

Knock-down (KDs)
   fasteners
Screwdriver
Drill and 20mm bit (or bit
   size recommended by
   KD manufacturer)
1½" drywall screws
1¼" panhead screws
¾"-thick melamine stock
   for 2 verticals and 3 or
   more shelves
Cardboard

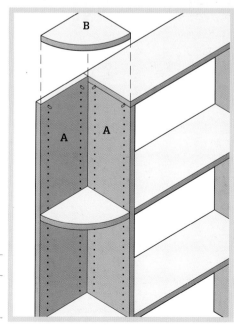

Key	Part	Dimension	Pcs.	Material
A	Verticals	14 × 84"	2	¾"-thick melamine shelving stock
B	Shelves	13½ × 14"	2	¾"-thick melamine shelving stock with curved front

Installing Wire Shelving

Wire shelving provides a quick and easy solution to a cluttered closet. It lacks adjustability but is nevertheless an inexpensive option to help organize your closet. Basic wire shelving is attached to walls with support brackets. For entire wall lengths we recommend finding a system that also has return wall brackets (often called "side wall brackets") and support clips (both drywall shelf clips and stud shelf clips are available at home centers). Support brackets placed at stud locations further stabilize the unit.

A slightly advanced style of wire shelving that is increasing in popularity is track-mounted and is available in more styles (other than standard white vinyl-coated wire shelving). This type of wire shelving consists of a horizontal rail track that supports vertical rails, or the vertical is directly fastened to the wall. Shelf brackets then snap into the verticals and shelves are set on top of the shelf supports. These systems are viable closet organizers but cannot bear as much weight as wood or melamine systems. The span should be kept to 36" or less and have adequate support—by hitting studs and using toggle bolts every 16".

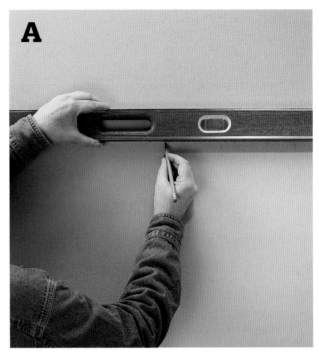

Measure your closet, and draw a level line 48" up from ground.

How to Install Wire Shelving

A. MEASURE WALLS AND MARK FOR SHELVING PLACEMENT

1. Measure the length of the back wall and the side walls.
2. Measure up from the ground to the desired height for the top shelf and draw a level line on each side wall. *Note: The average minimum height above ground is 48" (this allows for short-hang space and 12" clearance up from ground).*
3. Mark all stud locations along the back wall and side walls.

B. CUT WIRE SHELVING

Cut wire shelving to fit between walls using a hacksaw. For shelving lengths greater than 8 ft., cut multiple shelves and connect them with the manufacturer's connectors (which are often sold at home centers that carry wire shelving).

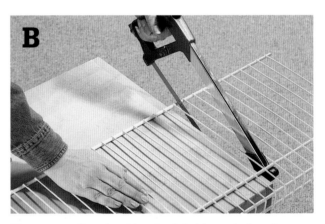

Measure and mark cut length of shelving onto the wire. Cut wire shelving to length, using a hacksaw.

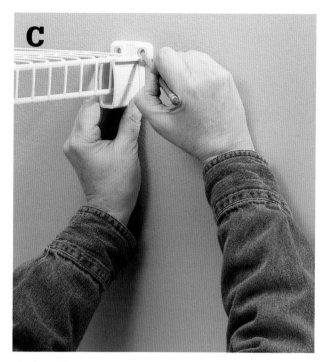

Fit the side-wall bracket in place on the wire shelf and then, holding the shelf in place along the level line on back wall, mark the screw hole placements for the support on the side wall.

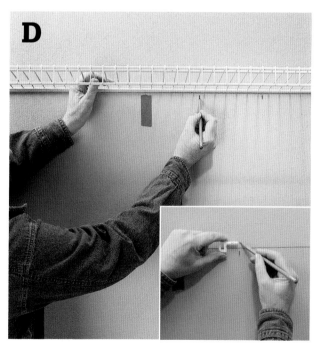

Mark the clip locations on center to spaces in wire and evenly between each stud mark. (Inset) Mark actual clip pin-hole placement according to manufacturer instructions.

C. ATTACH SIDE-WALL SUPPORTS

1. On a side wall, determine placement of the side-wall support according to manufacturer instructions. If instructions are not provided by the manufacturer, fit the support in place on the wire shelf and then, while holding the shelf in place along the level lines, mark the screw hole placements for the side-wall supports on the side walls.

2. Predrill holes at the marked side-wall support locations. Hold a support in place and insert a toggle bolt through the support into the wall. Repeat with the other side-wall support. *Note: If you can hit a stud, a toggle bolt is not necessary; instead, use a standard $1^1/2$" drywall screw.*

3. Place the wire shelving into the side-wall supports. Simply lower the shelving into place until it clicks into the supports. Have a helper hold the shelf so that the two side-wall brackets are not bearing the load of the shelf. Check for level.

D. MARK WALL FOR SUPPORT CLIPS

1. With wire shelving still fit into the sidewall supports from step C, make a mark approximately every 6" along the wall; evenly space the marks between studs, and on center to spaces in wire.

2. Remove the wire shelving. Hold a clip at each mark, according to manufacturer instructions, and mark the pin-hole location. *Note: There is an offset from the level line on the wall that must be taken into account.*

Tip ▸

For side walls that are at least 4 ft. deep, consider adding wire shelving along these walls that extend to the back walls. Then cut your back wall shelving to stop at the edges of these shelves (instead of extending all the way to the return walls). Special corner connectors are available at most home centers—they join the side wall shelving with the back wall shelving.

E

Predrill holes for the wall clips. (Inset) Insert the clip pins into predrilled holes, using a hammer to tap them into the wall, if necessary.

Fasten support brackets at studs.

E. PLACE THE SUPPORT CLIPS IN WALL

1. Predrill holes at the support clip marks on back wall for the pin-hole placement.
2. Insert the wall clips by pressing the manufacturer pin through the clip and into the wall. Use a hammer to tap stubborn pins into the wall.
3. Lower wire shelving into the side-wall supports until they snap into place.
4. Gently press the back of the shelving into the support clips.

F. ATTACH SUPPORT BRACKETS

1. Where possible, align support brackets at stud locations. Mark screw holes on wall.
2. Determine where the other brackets will go on the wall for a uniform appearance. Space brackets approximately every 16" apart along the back wall.
3. Attach wall brackets at stud marks, drilling screws through the bracket holes and into the anchors. For brackets that are not fastened to studs, use toggle bolts.
4. Fasten the other end of the brackets to the wire shelving according to the manufacturer instructions.

Metal Shelf ▶

There is a slightly different version of metal standards that is designed to screw directly to the wall. These are essentially vertical rails that support adjustable shelving brackets. Follow manufacturer recommendations for weight loads.

Mark a level line for the mounting height on the wall.

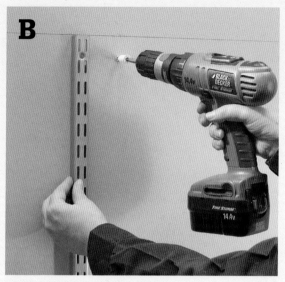

Where you cannot hit a stud, insert a self-driving wall anchor (like E-Z Ancors) into the wall (or predrill holes for toggle bolts).

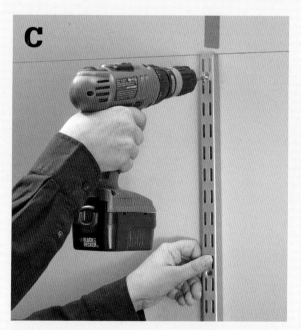

At stud marks, temporarily fasten a screw in the top of the metal standard. Plumb the rail and then screw to wall.

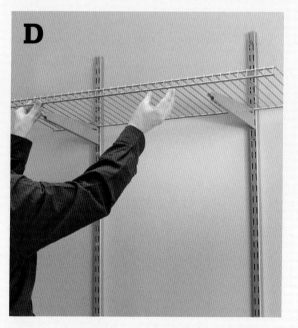

Screw rails to wall, and then add shelving brackets.

Installing a Basic Closet Organizer

This basic, traditional closet organizer was designed with a bedroom closet in mind, but it can be adapted for a pantry or entryway closet. With a custom-built central shelf unit, items such as shoes, blankets, and sweaters stay organized.

The two upper shelves are perfect for accessory items or seasonal clothing.

Best of all, you can build this organizer for a 5-foot closet for the cost of a single sheet of plywood, a clothes pole, and a few feet of 1 × 3 lumber.

Tools, Materials & Cutting List ▸

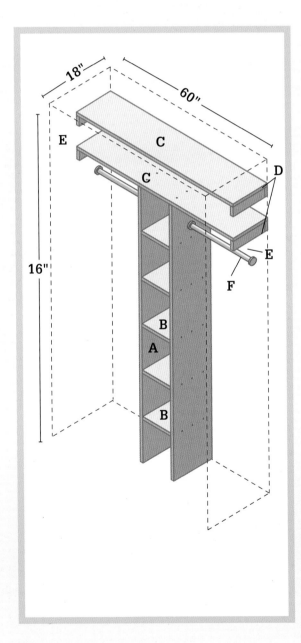

Hammer
Tape measure
Framing square
Circular saw
Screwdriver
Jigsaw
Level

6d and 8d finish nails
$\frac{3}{4}$" × 4 × 8' finish-grade plywood
$1\frac{1}{4}$"-dia. × 6' clothes pole
(2) 1 × 3" × 8' pine
(1) 1 × 3" × 6' pine
Clothes-pole brackets
Finish materials

Key	Part	Dimension	Pcs.	Material
A	Central shelf side	$\frac{3}{4} \times 11\frac{7}{8} \times 76$"	2	Plywood
B	Shelf	$\frac{3}{4} \times 11\frac{7}{8} \times 11\frac{7}{8}$"	5	Plywood
C	Upper shelf	$\frac{3}{4} \times 11\frac{7}{8}$" × 5'	2	Plywood
D	Back wall support	$\frac{3}{4} \times 2\frac{1}{2}$" × 5'	2	Pine
E	End wall support	$\frac{3}{4} \times 2\frac{1}{2} \times 20$"	4	Pine
F	Clothes pole	$1\frac{1}{4}$"-dia. × 6'	2	Closet Pole

How to Make a Basic Closet Organizer

Drive 8d finish nails through the supports into the wall studs.

Assemble the central shelving unit, leaving the top open.

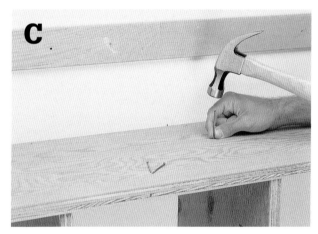

Install the upper shelves with 6d finish nails.

A. CUT & INSTALL WALL SUPPORTS

1. Cut the shelf supports for the two upper shelves to fit the dimensions of the closet.
2. Attach the supports to the wall so the top edges are 84 and 76" above the floor. Anchor the supports with 8d finish nails driven into wall studs.

B. ASSEMBLE THE CENTRAL SHELVING UNIT

1. Measure and cut the shelf sides and shelves to size.
2. Assemble the central shelf unit, using 6d finish nails. Space the shelves according to the height of the items you will store, but leave the top of the unit open.
3. Position the central shelf unit in the middle of the closet and use a pencil to mark notches at the top of each side to fit around the lower support.
4. Cut away the notched area with a jigsaw, and place the shelf against the back wall of the closet.

C. INSTALL THE UPPER SHELVES & CLOTHES POLE

1. Measure and cut the upper shelves to size.
2. Position one upper shelf on the lower shelf supports and the top of the central shelf unit. Attach it with 6d finish nails driven into the wall supports and the central shelf sides.
3. Lay the remaining upper shelf on the top shelf supports and attach it with 6d finish nails.
4. Attach pole brackets to the shelf unit, 11" from the rear wall and 3" below the upper shelf. Attach the opposing brackets to the walls. Make sure the brackets are attached to a stud in the closet wall, or use a wall anchor to attach it to the wallboard.

Installing a Basic Shelving Organizer

This simple project will more than double the storage potential in a small linen or pantry closet. It is perfect for light loads in closets with a span of 36" or less. The 1 × 3 furring strips are inexpensive and easy to install, and the shelving seen from the outside of the door lends a professional touch. If you don't have a lot of time, but would like to try your hand at an installation to maximize your storage, start here.

Tools & Materials ▶

Stud finder	¾"-thick shelving stock
Tape measure	(without predrilled
Level	holes)
Crewdriver	1 × 3 pine
Jigsaw	Wood screws
Nail gun	L-brackets (optional)
6d and 8d finish nails	Finish materials

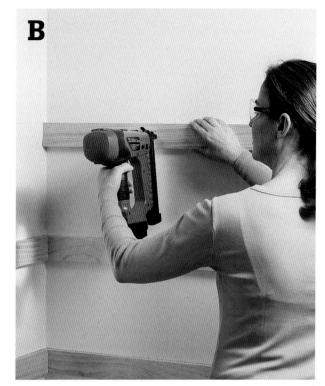

Measure from the floor up 15" and mark a level line. Repeat level lines every 12" up from original line (repeat four times for an 80"-tall closet).

Fasten 1 × 3 strips to back side wall, flush into each corner, and fasten 1 × 3 strips along the side wall (as shown, ending approximately 6" in from door track). Align the tops of 1 × 3 strips with level lines on wall and fasten to wall with a nail gun at studs. *Note: If you cannot hit a stud, use a self-driving metal anchor with machine screw every 10".*

How to Make a Basic Shelving Organizer

A. Measure from the floor up 15" and mark a level line. Repeat level lines every 12" up from original line (repeat four times for an 80"-tall closet).

B. Cut 1 × 3 strips to fit along the back wall, flush into each corner. Cut 1 × 3 strips to fit along side walls, flush against the back wall 1 × 3 strips and 4" short of inside wall (approximately 6" in from closet door track). Align the tops of 1 × 3 strips with level lines on wall and fasten to wall, hitting studs where possible. *Note: If you cannot hit a stud, use a self-driving metal anchor with machine screw every 10".*

C. Cut melamine shelving stock (without pre-drilled holes) to fit along back wall (measure wall and subtract 4"). Rest shelves on top of 1 × 3 strips.

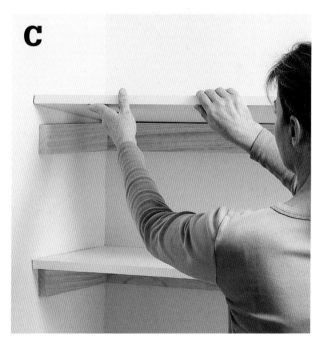

Cut melamine shelving stock (without predrilled holes) to fit along back wall (measure wall and subtract 4").

Rest shelves on top of 1 × 3 strips.

Custom Installations

Now that you have the basic techniques down, it's time to build your own custom closet. This section includes the step-by-step instructions for custom installations. Of course, your custom design will vary from our measurements, but the basic procedures will remain the same.

In this section:

- Installing a Wall-hung Unit
- Installing a Floor-based Unit
- Installing a Built-in
- New Closets

Installing a Wall-hung Unit

In a wall-hung system verticals with adjustable brackets are hung on a rail attached to the wall—the space along the floor remains open. Typically, the system is hung 87" from the floor and has a clearance of 4 to 6" from the finished floor.

There are two common methods to hang a wall-hung system. The traditional, premodular method requires a wall cleat or "nailer" that is mounted into the studs along the wall. The nailer is usually a 2 × 4 that spans the entire length of the wall. Cleats are attached to the underside of fixed top shelves.

The second method, which is used most frequently by closet professionals, uses a steel rail and adjustable rail brackets. The rail is mounted to studs and typically reinforced with toggle bolts (in hollow wall sections) along the entire wall. An adjustable bracket is attached to each vertical at the "rout-out" (an area on the vertical that is routed out to allow the vertical to fit over the rail and still be flush to the wall). Adjustable brackets help plumb verticals—even despite slightly irregular walls. While this method is desirable to closet professionals for its adjustability, flexibility, and ease of installation, such hanging rails and adjustable brackets are predominantly sold at specialty stores (see page 140).

Either way, nailer method or rail method, wall-hung systems are relatively easy to install and offer a host of advantages. One of the biggest benefits of a wall-hung system is versatility. Wall-hung systems can be mounted at any height on the wall. This flexibility gives the option to mount your system higher on the wall (ceiling height permitting), which is a big plus if you are tall. The reverse is true as well: if you are petite, you can mount the system closer to the floor. Also, having your system hang on the wall gives you floor access. If you decide to replace your carpet or flooring, the closet system will not interfere with removal or installation. Speaking of flooring, another advantage of a wall-hung system is that your closet will be level, even if your floor is not. This helps with an easy and fast installation.

Fixed shelves give stability to any modular system. In this project we affix shelves with KDs and KD screws, and then fasten them to the wall with steel L-brackets. Fixed shelves allow for other shelves in the unit to be fully adjustable without affecting the stability of the unit. The closet rail supporting this wall-hung unit will be hung with drywall screws and backed up with drywall anchors. *Note: Square, clean cuts are key when working with melamine closet shelving. This design maximizes your hanging space, and it also provides extra storage—including a shoe cubby, basket, and drawers.*

Tools & Materials ▸

Measuring tape	¾" panhead screws
Circular saw with melamine blade	Shelf pins
	Protective caps for closet rods
Router with straight bit	Euro or barrel screws
Clamps	Nails
20mm drill bit	Melamine shelving stock
Support cleats or L-brackets	(1) 8' hanging rail
Hacksaw	5 hanging brackets
Level (2 or 4')	36 KD fasteners with screws and dowels
Stud finder	(20) 2" drywall screws
Phillips screwdriver	
9" (Torpedo) level	
Drill	For nailer method:
Self-driving wall anchors (Buildex E-Z Ancors)	2 × 4 melamine nailer
	3½" drywall screws
2" drywall screws	T-square
	Jigsaw with a melamine blade

FLOOR PLAN - WALL HUNG

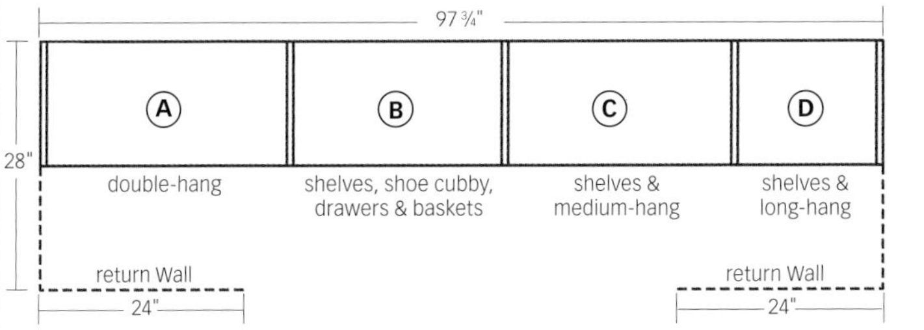

97 ¾"

28"

(A)	(B)	(C)	(D)
double-hang	shelves, shoe cubby, drawers & baskets	shelves & medium-hang	shelves & long-hang

return Wall
24"

return Wall
24"

Before & After Specs

Before:
- 96" hanging
- 96" shelving

After:
- 98" hanging
- 276" shelving

* Actual wall mounting height varies depending on size of hanging rail or nailer used. Always refer to manufacturer instructions. Fixed shelves highlighted.

ELEVATION PLAN - WALL HUNG

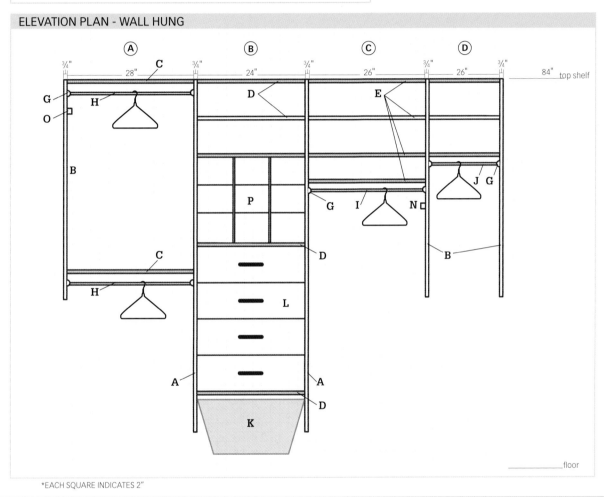

*EACH SQUARE INDICATES 2"

Cutting List

Key	Part	Dimension	Pcs.	Material
A	Verticals	76 ⁵⁄₁₆"	2	¾" Melamine
B	Verticals	47 ⅜"	3	¾" Melamine
C	Shelves	28" wide	2	¾" Melamine
D	Shelves	24" wide	5	¾" Melamine
E	Shelves	26" wide	4	¾" Melamine
F	Shelves	16" wide	3	¾" Melamine
G	Sets of rod cups	¼" thick	4	As desired
H	Rods	27 ¾"	2	As desired

Key	Part	Dimension	Pcs.	Material
I	Rod	25 ¾"	1	As desired
J	Rod	15 ¾"	1	As desired
K	Basket	24"	1	As desired
L	Drawers	24"	4	As desired
M	Shoe cubby	24"	1	¾" Melamine
N	Belt rack	Match unit depth	1	As desired
O	Tie rack	Match unit depth	1	As desired

*MOUNTING HEIGHT IS 80"

How to Make & Install a Wall-Hung Unit

Measure the return wall to determine the maximum shelf depth possible for your space.

Hold shelves in place using clamps and jigs. Cut your shelves to size using a circular saw with a melamine blade.

A. DETERMINE CLOSET DEPTH

1. Measure the return wall to determine the depth of the closet.
2. Determine the shelving depth. Refer back to the Design section, if needed (starting on page 29).

B. CUT SHELVES

Measure and mark ¾"-thick melamine to size according to the plans. *Note: 8-ft. shelf stock at 12, 14, or 16" depths (depending on your preferred depth for storage you determined in step A) will work for all cut pieces in this project.*

C. CUT & PREPARE VERTICALS

1. On precut shelving stock (at the desired depth), cut all verticals to length. *Alternative: If you intend to purchase melamine sheets to cut out your own verticals: measure and mark a sheet of ¾" melamine to the desired depth and length according to plans, using a square for accurate measurements. Remember to leave space in between each vertical for cut waste (determined by the saw blade thickness).*

2. Drill shelf-pin holes along the sides of the verticals. Align the center of the first two holes along the top of the vertical ⅜" down from the vertical top edge. This allows your verticals to have a flush top shelf. If the purchased shelf stock has predrilled holes along the inside for shelf pins, you can move on to step 3.

3. Mark the area to be "routed out" (a section of the vertical that is essentially cut out with a drill) for the hanging rail 4" down from the top, ¾" deep. If you're using a 2 × 4 nailer, the routed area must be 3½" tall and 1½" deep. *Note: Routing out the space is easier than cutting it; although, you can use a jigsaw with a melamine blade to get the job done.*

4. Clamp the vertical to a work table and rout out the verticals for hanging brackets along your marked pencil lines.

Rout out the verticals for hanging brackets according to the size and location of the hanging rail.

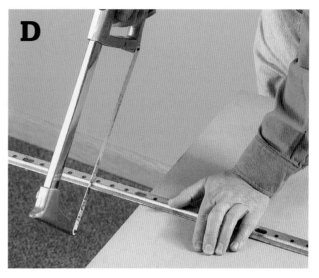

Cut the steel wall rail to size, using a hacksaw.

D. CUT RAIL

1. Measure wall-to-wall along the back wall to determine the length of rail you need.
2. Using a rail that you find at a specialty store, cut to size to span the length of the back wall, using a hacksaw.

E. MARK HANGING RAIL LOCATION

1. Draw a level line across the length of the wall at 80" off the floor. This height varies according to manufacturer instructions.
2. Locate and mark stud locations on wall, using a stud finder.
3. Holding the bottom of rail on wall at marked line, make marks through rail holes for wall anchor (or toggle bolt) locations in between each stud mark. Also mark rail holes at studs. Set the rail on the floor.
4. Predrill holes in the wall for wall anchors (or drive in toggle bolts) at marks in between studs.

F. FASTEN RAIL TO WALL

1. Hold the rail in place at center, press wall anchor into predrilled holes and lock into place.
2. Drive 2" drywall screws through rail and into wall at marked stud locations.
3. Snap on plastic rail cover according to manufacturer instructions.

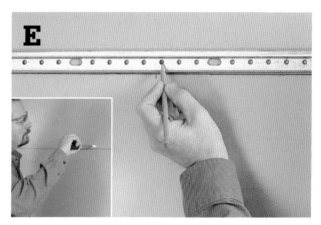

Hold the rail in place and make pencil marks through the mounting holes on the rail. (Inset) At marks that do not hit studs, predrill holes and then drive in E-Z Ancors.

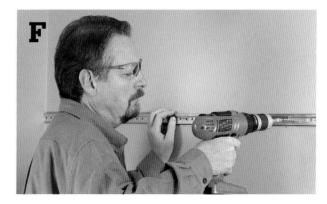

Drill 2" stud screws through rail and into wall at marked locations.

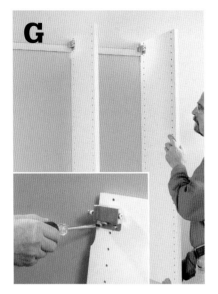

G

H

I

Secure rail brackets to verticals on center at your pre-drilled locations with Euro or barrel screws (Inset). Hang all verticals on rail at desired locations along the entire wall.

Mark locations to predrill holes for KDs on top shelf on center to predrilled holes on verticals.

Using a Phillips screwdriver, "lock down" your fixed shelves.

G. ATTACH BRACKETS TO VERTICALS

1. Predrill ⅛" holes on center of routout section on verticals for the rail brackets. *Note: If your shelves have predrilled shelf-pin holes, some manufacturer brackets fasten directly into the shelf-pin holes with Euro screws or barrel screws. Be sure to check manufacturer instructions.*

2. Attach adjustable rail brackets to the verticals according to manufacturer instructions, using ¾" panhead screws.

3. Hang all verticals on hanging rail according to plans. The hook of the bracket should hang over the rail (and plastic rail cover).

H. PREPARE FIXED SHELVES

1. Align the fixed shelves tops flush with vertical tops.

2. Mark the center of shelf-pin holes onto underside of fixed shelves.

3. Drill for KDs at marks on underside of fixed shelves, using the bit size recommended by the manufacturer. Set back from shelf edges based on KD size and manufacturer instructions. See recommendations in Resources (page 140).

4. Press KDs into the drilled holes on underside of shelf.

I. ATTACH FIXED SHELVES

1. Fasten KD screws and dowels (see photo) through verticals according to where fixed shelves will sit (refer to the plans for this specific project). The screws and dowels should fit directly into predrilled shelf-pin holes.

2. Using a Phillips screwdriver, "lock down" your fixed shelves (attach all fixed shelves with KDs fitting over KD screws on verticals) in the first section. KDs only require 20 lbs. of force and a clockwise turn of 180°. Continue to do this until all sections are complete. *Note: If a single vertical supports a fixed shelf on either side of it, use a screw and dowel (instead of two screws), so they can lock together.*

J. ADJUST FOR PLUMB AND LEVEL

1. Level all horizontal shelves using a 9" (Torpedo) level. Adjust as necessary.

2. Starting at the far left, plumb each vertical using a level. Use screw adjustments on mounting brackets to bring vertical as close to the wall as possible; and then adjust in and out, up and down as necessary for a level unit and even spacing between sections. Continue to adjust the verticals until everything is plumb. As you adjust for plumb, be sure to double-check the shelves for level.

Adjust the verticals for plumb by simply adjusting the hanging rail according to manufacturer instructions. Adjustments can slightly lift verticals or push them away from the wall. With this adjustability you can move along the entire wall until your closet unit is perfectly plumb, despite irregular walls.

Align L-brackets with back of wall and fixed shelves. Attach to the shelf with ¾" panhead screws and attach to the wall at stud locations with 2" stud screws. *Note: If your shelves have wood cleats already attached to them, simply fasten them to the wall with 3" screws.*

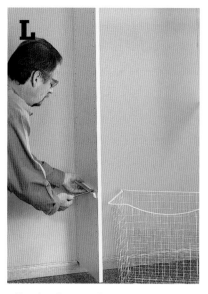

Align basket tracks over predrilled holes. Fasten the track at predrilled holes with Euro or barrel screws. Slide the basket onto the track according to manufacturer instructions.

K. SECURE UNIT IN PLACE

1. Once the entire unit is level and plumb, align steel L-brackets flush with wall and underside of fixed shelves (see plans on page 75 for suggested fixed locations).
2. Screw the L-bracket into the wall at stud locations with 2" screws—or use screws driven into hollow wall anchors where there are no studs. Screw the L-bracket to the shelf with ¾" panhead screws.
   Alternative: If your fixed shelves have wood cleats attached to them, simply screw them into the wall with 3" drywall screws.

L. ADD FINISHING TOUCHES

For specifics on adding accessories, refer to the Accessories section starting on page 103.

1. Insert shelf pins on verticals where desired. Place adjustable shelves onto pins.
2. Mark the locations for closet rods on verticals per plans. Attach end caps at marked locations. Place the rods into cups. If necessary, use a hacksaw or chop saw to cut metal rods to fit. Place protective caps over the cut ends before placing back into the rod cups on the verticals.

3. Install pre-built drawers by screwing drawer tracks onto the verticals using Euro or barrel screws aligned with shelf pins. Slide drawers into place, adjust as necessary for level and for uniform gaps in between drawers.
4. Install pre-assembled baskets. Screw basket tracks onto verticals according to manufacturer instructions. Slide the basket onto the track and level or adjust as necessary.
5. Slide your prebuilt shoe cubby onto the shelf directly above drawers. Or fasten vertical partitions in place according to design by countersinking nails through the top shelf into the top of prepared verticals. Insert shelf pins where desired and slide adjustable shelves into place.
6. Add your tie and belt racks (refer to pages 108 and 109), by attaching them to the sides of verticals with Euro or barrel screws aligned with shelf-pin holes.

Tip ▸

If KDs do not press easily into the predrilled holes, tap them into place using a rubber mallet.

Alternative: How to Use a Wood Nailer System

Drill 3" wood screws through the rail at studs and run screws to fit into the drywall anchors you chose at non-stud locations.

Cut a notch in the vertical to fit around the 2 × 4 nailer, allowing the vertical to sit flush to the wall.

A helper may come in handy with this procedure. This is another reason why closet professionals prefer a rail system. With nailers each section must be fully assembled before moving to the next. And it's difficult to hold the verticals in place while also locking down KDs.

A. INSTALL NAILER

1. Cut 2 × 4 melamine nailer to width of wall-to-wall measurement, using a circular saw with a melamine blade. If your wall-to-wall measurement is greater than 5 ft., cut multiple nailers that butt up next to one another on the wall.
2. Locate and mark stud locations on wall.
3. Draw a level line 77" up from the floor for the top of the nailer.
4. Hold the top of the nailer flush with the marked line.
5. Predrill holes for 3½" drywall screws at your stud marks on the wall. In between each stud mark, drive in a self-driving wall anchor.

6. Holding the nailer in place, countersink 3" drywall screws through the cleat and into the predrilled holes in studs. In between each stud, drive screws into the self-drilling wall anchors.

B. CUT NOTCH IN VERTICALS

Verticals must still be fitted with pin-style holes for KDs and adjustable shelf pins. See page 46 for instructions on drilling pin holes, or purchase shelf stock with predrilled holes and cut to the appropriate height. Remember to measure ⅜" on center to a pin hole from top edge to ensure correct placement of KDs for top fixed shelf.

1. Mark a square notch on the wall-side edge of the vertical. Draw a line 3½" down from the top. Draw another line 3½" down from the first line. Connect the two lines using a T-square at 1½" deep (you may need to measure the exact depth of the 2 × 4 so the vertical will sit flush to the wall).

Align verticals and fasten fixed shelves in the first section. Check for plumb and level before screwing the end vertical to the wall. Repeat with each section as you move along the wall.

2. Cut out the notch using a jigsaw with a melamine blade. *Note: This time the cuts on the vertical are square (opposed to wall-hung verticals on a rail system that are routed out with a drill) because they will be resting directly on the nailer. By this point fixed shelves should be fastened to cleats—see page 49. There must be a fixed shelf at the top, middle, and bottom of each section. You can add more fixed shelves, as needed, for structural support at locations intended to carry more weight.*

C. INSTALL THE CLOSET

1. Holding a corner vertical in place so that the notch fits snugly around the nailer, temporarily fasten the vertical to the wall with a 3½" screw centered toward the top of the vertical. *Note: Verticals do not support systems that use nailers. The nailers are simply guides to help with holding verticals in place as fixed shelves are attached, and to maintain a level unit. The fixed shelves with cleats screwed to the wall are what ultimately hold these systems in place. The end verticals are also screwed to the wall along the top, middle, and bottom.*

2. Lower the top fixed shelf into place and lock down KDs to vertical on wall. The shelf cleat should sit flush with the nailer.

3. Hold a second vertical over the nailer and lock down KDs to that vertical.

4. Plumb and level the unit, and then permanently fasten the end vertical to the wall.

5. Check level of top and shelf, and adjust as necessary. Once level, screw the shelf cleat into the wall with either two or three 3" screws evenly spaced.

6. Finish attaching the rest of the fixed shelves in between these two verticals.

7. Repeat the above procedure for the next section along the wall. Once all sections have verticals in place and fixed shelf cleats fastened to the wall, add adjustable shelves.

Installing a Floor-based Unit

A floor-based system typically extends 90" up from the finished floor. The most obvious advantage is support—and the strong, stable support is the floor. Even though wall-hung systems (if installed correctly) are strong, floor-based systems are worry-free. Because, you don't have to worry about them falling, you can build deeper components, such as drawer sections, and add more weight. Typical closet systems, both wall-hung and floor-based, are 12 to 14" deep. However, if you have a big enough closet, it is nice to build drawers and shelving deeper to really maximize your storage.

Some people are also attracted to floor-based units because of the option to add features to the unit to mimic a built-in—most notably base molding, crown molding, and wall trim.

If you would like toe-kick molding on the bottom of your unit, you have two options: 1.) Make and install a thin backer board and slide it into place in between verticals; often installers will fasten this to verticals on the inside with L-brackets, and then install a lower shelf directly on top to conceal the insert. 2.) Install a kickbase at the start of the project. Simply make the kickbase 3¾" shorter than the depths of the verticals to allow for a lip at the bottom of the unit. Align verticals to rest half on the kickbase, concealing the kickbase from the side as well as the front. Install the unit as if this platform is the floor—taking all measurements up from the kickbase. Be sure the kickbase is level, despite an irregular or sloping floor.

For all cut pieces in this project, 8-ft. shelf stock at 12, 14, 16, or 24" depth (depending on your preferred depth for storage) will work.

Tools & Materials ▸

Measuring tape	¾"-thick melamine
4" level	shelving stock with
Circular saw with	predrilled holes
melamine blade	¾"-thick melamine
Drill	board (or shelving
20 mm drill bit	stock without
Rubber mallet	predrilled holes)
L-brackets	Wood shims
Stud finder	Melamine glue
Phillips screwdriver	Shims
Level	Locking KD with
3" drywall screws	screws and screw/
2" drywall screws	dowels

ELEVATION PLAN - Floor-based Unit

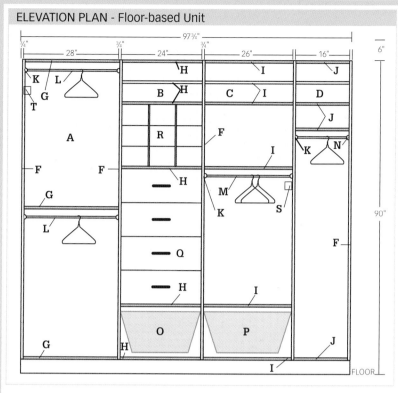

Kick-base

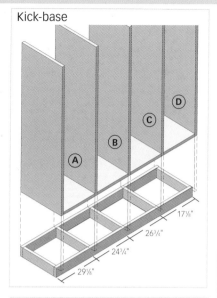

FLOOR PLAN - Floor-based Unit

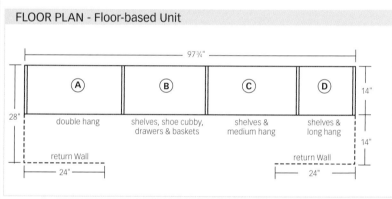

A — double hang
B — shelves, shoe cubby, drawers & baskets
C — shelves & medium hang
D — shelves & long hang

return Wall

97¾"
28"
14"
14"
24"
24"

Alternative Kick-base

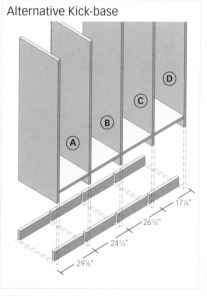

Cutting List

Key	Part	Dimension	Pcs.	Material
A	Kickbase	4 × 29⅛"	2	¾"-thick melamine
B	Kickbase	4 × 24¾"	2	¾"-thick melamine
C	Kickbase	4 × 26¾"	2	¾"-thick melamine
D	Kickbase	4 × 17⅛"	2	¾"-thick melamine
E	Kickbase	4 × (vertical depth minus 3¾")	5	¾"-thick melamine
F	Verticals	85⅜"	5	¾"-thick melamine
G	Shelves	28" wide	3	¾"-thick melamine
H	Shelves	24" wide	6	¾"-thick melamine
I	Shelves	26" wide	5	¾"-thick melamine
J	Shelves	16" wide	4	¾"-thick melamine

Key	Part	Dimension	Pcs.	Material
K	Rod cups	¼" thick	4	As desired
L	Rods	27¾"	2	As desired
M	Rod	25¾"	1	As desired
N	Rod	15¾"	1	As desired
O	Basket	24"	1	As desired
P	Basket	26"	1	As desired
Q	Drawers	24"	4	As desired
R	Shoe cubby	24"	1	As desired
S	Belt rack with Euro screws		1	As desired
T	Tie/scarf rack with Euro screws		1	As desired

How to Make and Install a Floor-based Unit

OPTION: MAKE TOE-KICK BASE

1. Cut ¾"-thick melamine shelf stock (without shelf-pin holes) to 4" wide by the desired length for front and back kickbase plates (see cut list on page 83).
2. Then cut side kickbase plates at 4"-wide by (vertical depth minus 3¾").
3. Align the front and back plates for the first section flush with the inside edges of the side plates. Align the inner side on center to the edges of the front and back plates.
4. Drive a screw through the back plate and into the sides; then use L-brackets to secure the front plate to the sides.
5. Move to the next section, adding another side plate. Continue this until the entire kickbase is complete.
6. Align kickbase in between verticals, so that half the vertical is resting on kickbase and other half overhangs kickbase.
7. Level the kickbase by inserting shims under verticals, as needed. *Alternative: Extend each vertical to the floor and use L-brackets to fasten kickbase plates in between each vertical.*

A. MEASURE THE CLOSET

1. Draw a level line 90" above the floor.
2. Lay out the verticals onto the wall as shown in the plans.
3. At each vertical location, measure from the level line to the floor to determine the total length of the vertical.
4. *Note: If floor slopes from the wall out, you can cut the end of the verticals at an angle or shim the side where the floor is lowest. Look for significant inconsistencies of ⅛" or greater. A framing square set against the wall and floor will tell you whether the floor slopes (or the wall is out of plumb).*
5. Using a stud finder, mark all stud locations along the installation wall.

B. PREPARE VERTICALS

Cut all verticals to length depending on design. In this project they are 87 ⅝" tall. *Note: All verticals are cut to ⅜" on center of holes. This allows your verticals to have a flush top shelf (see page 46).*

Measure up 90" from the floor every foot or so and make an X. Then draw a level line across the walls. Compare these marks to determine if your floor is level along the wall.

Mark your cutline on the verticals, using a carpenter's square to ensure a straight cutline at right angles to the edges. Be sure to leave room for waste from the saw fence.

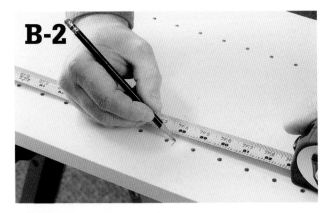

Measure verticals to be 87 ⅝" long. From on center of shelf-peg holes add ⅜" and make a mark. The offset of ⅜" allows for the Knock-down screws to fit into the predrilled holes while in KDs, allowing the top shelf to sit flush with the top of verticals.

C. INSTALL CLOSET

1. Start with the farthest left vertical. Predrill an angled pilot hole drilled through the vertical.
2. Place the vertical in position against wall and use a level to make sure it is perfectly plumb. Screw the vertical to the wall with a 2" drywall screw located at center to hold piece temporarily in place.
3. Screw in locking KD dowels on the verticals at fixed shelf locations. *Note: The KD dowels are placed on center of predrilled shelf-pin holes. This allows an accurate fit of the KD over the dowel and flush front edges. The bottom fixed shelf attaches in the second hole from the bottom (approximately 2" from floor).*
4. Using a Phillips screwdriver, attach all fixed shelves with KDs fitting over KD dowels on verticals. Continue to do this until all sections are complete.

D. PREPARE FIXED SHELVES

1. Follow the plans to cut materials.
2. Measure and mark your shelf sizes onto the shelf stock according to the plan sizes. Check for square.
3. Cut your shelves to size using a circular saw with a melamine blade.
4. On your fixed shelves, mark for KD holes "on center" to shelf-pin holes on verticals.
5. Drill for KDs on the fixed shelves, using 20mm drill bit or the bit size recommended by the manufacturer.
6. Tap KDs into place on fixed shelves using a rubber mallet.

OPTION: ADD MOUNTING CLEATS TO FIXED SHELVES

Fixed shelves are often fixed to the wall with steel brackets at the end of the installation. If you prefer to have shelf cleats under the fixed shelves, you would prepare them now. Shelf cleats add a different aesthetic feel and look to the closet, and this is the main reason for making them instead of using steel L-brackets. Here's how to prepare the fixed shelves with cleats:

1. Using ¾" melamine, rip cut cleats to 3½" wide.
2. Cut to width of shelves based on cut list.
3. Glue and pin-nail cleat to underside of the fixed shelf, flush with the back (wall side).

Align the first vertical against the wall and temporarily screw it to the wall.

Tap KDs in to place on fixed shelves using a rubber mallet.

Option: Fasten the cleat to the underside of the fixed shelf using glue and pin-nails.

Level the entire unit and all of the shelves.

Add Shims under verticals, where necessary, to keep shelves level.

Plumb the entire unit, checking all verticals with a level.

Add accessories and adjustable shelves to build out the unit. Fasten L-brackets to fixed shelves.

E. PLUMB AND LEVEL UNIT

1. Once all fixed shelves are in place, level the unit. Be sure to level across the tops of the verticals and make sure the verticals are all square to outside walls.
2. Check the verticals for plumb. Move from section to section, plumbing and leveling the unit.

F. ADD SHIMS

For verticals that are too low due to a dip in the floor, use wood shims to raise them up to level. Once the appropriate height is achieved, slide a shim under the verticals. Tap the shim with a hammer, if needed.

G. FINISHING TOUCHES

1. Check each fixed shelf for level, and then secure the shelf to the wall with steel L-brackets. Align the L-bracket so it is pressed up tight against the bottom of the shelf, and then fasten it to the wall with 2" drywall screws. *Note: If you prepared fixed shelves with cleats, run 3" drywall screws through the mounting cleats into wall studs.*
2. Add adjustable shelves using shelf pins.
3. Install closet rods (see page 104) at locations per plans.
4. Install pre-built drawers (see page 110) by first screwing drawer tracks onto the verticals and then the edges of the drawer boxes.
5. Slide the drawers onto tracks. Adjust as necessary.
6. Screw basket tracks onto verticals and attach to the basket (refer to page 129). Slide basket into place.
7. Slide prebuilt shoe cubby (see page 106) onto shelf above drawers.
8. Add your tie and belt racks by holding the rack in place, insert Euro screws through the rack holes and directly into the shelf-pin holes on the vertical.

Using a pneumatic nailer, fasten crown molding in place along top front edges of closet unit.

Attach decorative molding by driving screws through the underside of the shelf up into the molding.

H. ADD CROWN MOLDING

1. Make light pencil marks at joist locations along edge of closet top shelf. For each piece that starts or ends in a corner, add 12 to 24" to compensate for waste. Avoid pieces shorter than 36", because short pieces are more difficult to cut.

2. Hold a section of molding against the closet and ceiling in the finished position. Make light pencil marks on the closet every 12" along the bottom edge of the molding. Remove the molding, and tack a finish nail at each mark. The nails will hold the molding in place while the adhesive dries.

3. To make miter cuts for the first corner, position the molding faceup in a miter box. Set the ceiling side of the molding against the horizontal table of the miter box, and set the wall side against the vertical back fence. Make the cut at 45°.

4. Check the uncut ends of each molding piece before installing. Make sure mating pieces butt together squarely in a tight joint. Cut all square ends at 90°, using a miter saw or hand miter box.

5. Run a bead of polymer adhesive along both edges.

6. Set the molding in place with the mitered end tight to the corner and the bottom edge resting on the nails. Attach the molding with a few nails (6d or 8d) driven through the flats and into the ceiling and wall, using a pneumatic nailer.

7. Cut and glue the next pieces of molding. Apply a bead of adhesive to each end where the installed molding will meet the new piece. Install each new piece, and secure the ends with screws, making sure the ends are joined properly.

8. Countersink all nails using a nail set. Use wood putty to fill visible nail holes and cover gaps at the joints.

I. ADD DECORATIVE MOLDING

1. Measure and cut a piece of decorative molding to fit in between two verticals in front of shoe shelves. Be sure to cut for a tight fit.

2. Attach molding to shelf by driving 1" screws from the underside of the shelf up into the bottom of the molding. *Note: Screw size is determined by shelf and molding base thickness.*

Installing a Built-In Organizer

A built-in closet system offers a finished, elegant appearance. You can give modular melamine closets the appearance of a built-in by adding trim, but for a true built-in many people prefer the look of natural wood.

This project uses finish-grade oak plywood and a solid oak face frame to give the unit the look of expensive, solid oak shelving—at a fraction of the cost. The plywood panels are supported and strengthened by an internal framework of 2 × 4 stud lumber.

When installing floor-to-ceiling shelves in a corner, as shown here, add 1/2" plywood spacers to add thickness to the studs that adjoin the wall. Spacers ensure that face frame stiles of equal width can be installed at both shelf ends (see diagram, opposite page). Before proceeding, first determine how you will design the built-in to fit into the corners (for walk-ins) so you can plan each built-in section along each wall accordingly (see page 50).

Tools & Materials ▶

Shims
Wood screws
    (1¾, 2, 3")
1½" finish nails
Metal shelf standards
    and clips
Finishing materials
½" plywood scraps
Molding (as desired)
Tape measure
Level
Framing square
Plumb bob
Drill
Hammer

Circular saw
Router
¾" straight bit
Flat prybar
Stud finder
Marking gauge

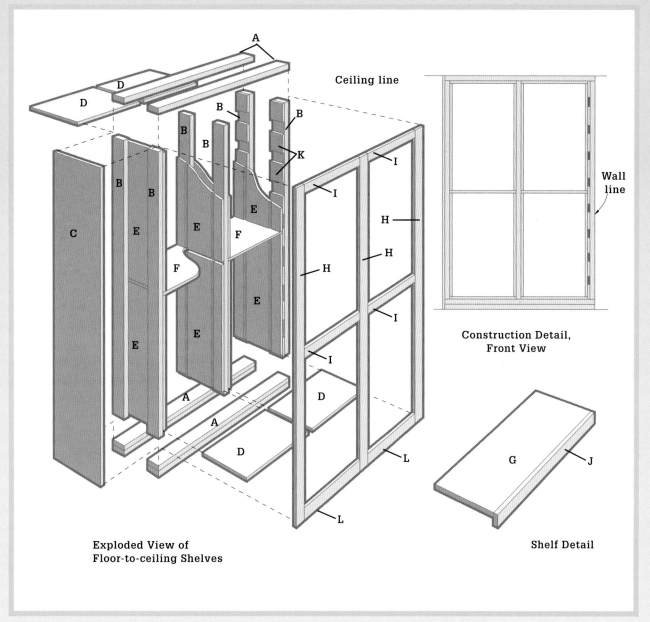

Exploded View of Floor-to-ceiling Shelves

Construction Detail, Front View

Shelf Detail

Note: Plan instructions are for one wall section. The dimensions of an entire built-in are dependent on your closet space. The same basic construction process as this example may be followed to achieve a complete walk-in built-in.

Key	Part	Dimension
A	(6) Top and sole plate	$1\frac{1}{2} \times 3\frac{1}{2} \times 59\frac{1}{2}$" pine
B	(6) Support stud	$1\frac{1}{2} \times 3\frac{1}{2} \times 91\frac{1}{2}$" pine
C	(1) End panel	$\frac{1}{2} \times 95\frac{3}{4} \times 13$" oak plywood
D	(4) Top, bottom panel	$\frac{1}{2} \times 27\frac{1}{4} \times 13$" oak plywood
E	(8) Upper, lower riser	$\frac{1}{2} \times 44\frac{7}{8} \times 13$" oak plywood
F	(2) Permanent shelf	$\frac{3}{4} \times 27\frac{1}{4} \times 13$" oak plywood

Key	Part	Dimension
G	(6) Adjustable shelf	$\frac{3}{4} \times 26\frac{1}{8} \times 13$" oak plywood
H	(3) Stile	$\frac{3}{4} \times 3\frac{1}{2} \times$ Cut to fit oak
I	(4) Top, middle rail	$\frac{3}{4} \times 2\frac{1}{2} \times 16\frac{1}{8}$" oak
J	(6) Shelf edging	$\frac{3}{4} \times 1\frac{1}{2} \times 26\frac{1}{8}$" oak
K	(16) Spacer	$\frac{1}{2} \times 3\frac{1}{2} \times 6$" oak
L	(2) Bottom rail	$\frac{3}{4} \times 3\frac{1}{2} \times 16\frac{1}{8}$" oak

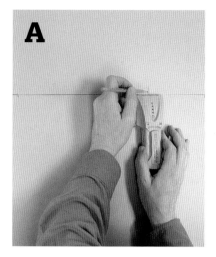

Locate studs on installation walls, using a stud finder.

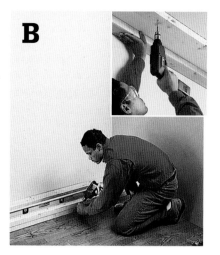

Use a plumb bob suspended from the outside corners of the top plates to align the sole plates. (Inset) Attach each plate to the ceiling with 3" screws driven into the joists or blocking.

Attach the plywood top and bottom panels to the top and sole plates using 1½" finish nails.

A. PREPARE THE WORK AREA

1. Detach and roll back carpeting and pad before beginning construction, then trim to fit around the built-in after work is completed. *Note: Install the built-in on top of glued-down carpeting.*
2. Remove baseboards and other moldings to make room for a built-in that will fit flush against the wall. Use a flat prybar with a wood block to prevent damage to the wall, and pry carefully to avoid splintering the molding. After the built-in is installed, cut the molding to size, and reattach it.
3. If electrical receptacles or other fixtures are in the way of your planned built-in, have them relocated by an electrician.
4. Use a stud finder to mark all of the studs on the installation walls.

B. INSTALL SUPPORT PLATES

1. Mark the location for two parallel 2 × 4 top plates on the ceiling, using a framing square as a guide. The front edge of the outer top plate should be 13" from back wall, and the other top plate should be flush against the wall. Mark location of ceiling joists; if necessary, install blocking between joists to provide a surface for anchoring the top plates.
2. Measure and cut 2 × 4 top plates. Position each plate, check to make sure it is level, and shim if necessary. Attach plates to ceiling with 3" screws driven into the joists or blocking.
3. Cut 2 × 4 sole plates and screw them together to form two doubled sole plates. Use a plumb bob suspended from the outside corners of the top plates to align the sole plates, then shim to level, if needed; anchor the plates by driving 3" screws toenailed into the floor.

C. INSTALL SUPPORT STUDS & END PANELS

1. Install 2 × 4 support studs between the ends of the top plates and sole plates. Attach support studs with 3" screws toenailed into the top plates and sole plates.
2. Install center support studs midway between the end support studs. Toenail to the bottom plate first, using 3" screws. Use a level to make sure that the stud is plumb, then attach the studs to the top plate with 3" screws.
3. Where the shelves fit into a corner, use 2" screws to attach ½" plywood spacers on the inside faces of the support studs, spaced every 4". Make sure the spacers do not extend past the front face of the studs.
4. Where the end of the project is exposed, measure and cut a ½" plywood end panel to floor-to-ceiling height. Attach the panel to the support studs so the front edges are flush, using 1¾" screws driven through the support studs and into the end panel.
5. Measure and cut ½" plywood top and bottom panels to fit between the support studs. Attach to the top and sole plates using 1½" finish nails.

Install the lower risers on each side of the 2 × 4 support studs with 1½" finish nails.

D. INSTALL RISERS AND PERMANENT SHELVES

1. Measure and cut lower risers from ½" plywood.
2. Mark two parallel dado grooves on the inside face of each riser, using a marking gauge. Grooves should be at least 1" from the edges.
3. Cut dadoes to depth and thickness of metal standards, using a router. Test-fit standards to make sure they fit, then remove them.
4. Install lower risers on each side of the 2 × 4 support studs so the front edges are flush with the edges of the studs. Attach risers with 1½" finish nails driven through the risers and into the support studs. For riser that adjoins wall, drive nails at spacer locations.
5. Measure and cut permanent shelves from ¾" plywood to fit between the support studs, just above the lower risers. Set shelves on risers and attach them with 1½" finish nails driven down into the risers.
6. Measure and cut upper risers to fit between the permanent shelves and the top panels. Cut dadoes for metal shelf standards, then attach the risers to the support studs with 1½" finish nails.

E. INSTALL FACING

1. Measure and cut 1 × 4 stiles to reach from floor to ceiling along the front edges of the exposed support studs. Drill pilot holes and attach the stiles to the support studs so they are flush with the risers, using glue and 1½" finish nails driven at 8" intervals into the studs and risers.

Measure and cut the 1 × 3 top rails to fit between the stiles. Then drill pilot holes and attach the rails to the top plate and top panels.

Insert shelf clips into the metal shelf standards and install the adjustable shelves.

2. Measure and cut 1 × 3 top rails to fit between the stiles. Drill pilot holes and attach the rails to the top plate and top panels, using glue and 1½" finish nails.
3. Measure and cut 1 × 4 bottom rails to fit between the stiles. Drill pilot holes, and attach the rails to the sole plates and bottom panels, using glue and 1½" finish nails. The top edge of the rails should be flush with the top surface of the plywood panels.
4. Fill nail holes, then sand and finish the wood surfaces as desired.

F. INSTALL SHELVING

1. Measure, cut, and install metal shelf standards into the dadoes, using nails or screws provided by the manufacturer.
2. Measure and cut adjustable shelves ⅛" shorter than the distance between metal standards. Cut shelf edging, and attach with glue and 1½" finish nails. Sand and finish the shelves as desired.
3. Insert shelf clips into metal shelf standards and install the adjustable shelves at desired heights.
4. Cover gaps between the project and walls and floor with molding that has been finished to match the shelf unit.

New Closets: Building a Walk-in Closet

Building a partition wall is a great way to downsize a room and get extra closet space at the same time. This is a perfect solution for guest rooms that are too large or largely empty throughout the year. Why sacrifice your closet storage for an empty room? Consider making that extra room cozier by taking half of the space for a reach-in or walk-in closet, thus getting double your use of the space.

Converting a room into a multi-functional room and closet opens other creative possibilities. Consider dedicating the room as a dressing or sitting area complete with a vanity dresser, large mirrors, and lounge furniture. The possibilities are endless, so let yourself dream up the best use for the space.

A partition wall divides an open space into two spaces but does not carry significant structural weight. If you're adding a wall to a current living space, you'll want to hang plastic around your project area to contain dust and debris.

Tools & Materials ▸

Drill	150-grit sandpaper or
Stud finder	sanding sponge
Circular saw	2 × 4 framing lumber
Chalk line	8d casing nails
Tape measure	10d and 16d common
Combination square	nails
Framing square	1¼" wallboard screws
Ladder	Premixed wallboard
Plumb bob	compound
Wallboard T-square	Paper wallboard tape
Wallboard saw	½" wallboard
4 or 6" and 10"	Bucket or pan
Wallboard knives	Prehung door kit
Utility knife	Hammer
	Wallboard lifter

How to Build a New Closet

A. LAY OUT THE WALL PLATES

1. Mark the location of the new wall on the ceiling and then snap two chalk lines to outline the position of the new top plate.
2. Use a stud finder to determine the location and direction of the joists. Mark the first joist and then drill into the ceiling between the lines. If your first joist mark was accurate, then measure to find the remaining joists.
3. Make the top and sole plates by cutting two 2 × 4s to length. Lay the plates side by side, and use a combination square to outline the stud locations at 16" intervals.
4. Mark the position of the door framing members on the top plate and sole plate, using Xs for king studs and Os for jack studs. Most prehung doors are 32" wide, but other sizes are available. Be sure to frame according to the prehung door unit and materials you plan to use. The rough opening measured between the insides of jack studs should be about 1" wider than the actual width of the door unit to allow for adjustments during installation.

Mark the location of the new wall with chalk lines and mark the first joist location. Drill into the ceiling to ensure your marks hit a joist.

Tip ▶

Walk-in closets vary in size but should have a minimum depth of 5 feet to allow a door to swing inward and still leave room for clothing to hang on the back wall. Return walls should be at least 24" to allow hanging on side walls.

Warning ▶

Before starting the project, check for wiring and plumbing in ceiling, walls, and floor in the area of the new wall.

Sidebar ▶

New wall perpendicular to joists: Attach the top plate and sole plate directly to the ceiling and floor joists with 16d nails.

New wall parallel to joists, but not aligned: Install 2 × 4 blocking between the joists every 2 feet, using 16d nails. The bottom of the blocking should be flush with the edges of joists. Anchor plates with 16d nails driven into the blocking.

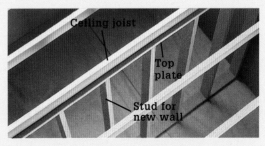

New wall aligned with parallel joists: Attach top plate to ceiling joist and sole plate to the floor, using 10d nails.

After tacking the top plate in place on ceiling, use a framing square to make sure the top plate is perpendicular to the adjoining walls.

B. INSTALL THE TOP AND SOLE PLATES

1. Position the top plate against the ceiling between the chalk lines, and use two nails to tack it in place with the stud marks facing down. Use a framing square to make sure the plate is perpendicular to the adjoining walls and then anchor the plate to the joists or blocking with 16d nails.
2. Determine the position of the sole plate by hanging a plumb bob from the edge of the top plate near an adjoining wall so the plumb bob tip nearly touches the floor. When the plumb bob is motionless, mark its position on the floor. Repeat at the opposite end of the top plate. Snap a chalk line between the marks to show the location of the sole plate.
3. Cut away the sole plate where the door framing will fit, then position the pieces of the sole plate on the outline on the floor. On wood floors, anchor the sole plate pieces with 16d nails driven into the floor joists.
4. Find the length of the first stud by measuring the distance between the sole plate and the top plate with a tape measure at the first stud mark. Cut the stud to length.

C. POSITION WALL STUDS

1. Position the stud between the top plate and sole plate so the stud markings are covered.
2. Attach the stud by toenailing through the sides of the stud into the top plate and then the sole plate, using 10d nails or 3" screws.
3. Measure, cut, and install all remaining full-length studs, one at a time. *Option: Attach studs to the top and sole plates with metal connectors and 4d nails.*

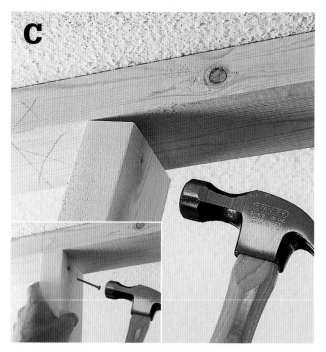

Position and attach stud by toenailing through the sides of the stud and into the top plate and then the sole plate.

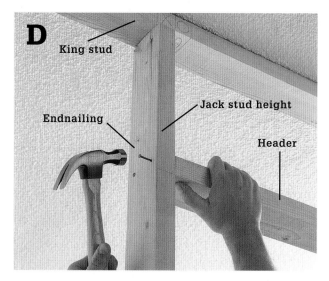

Endnail the header to the king stud above the mark for the jack stud.

D. INSTALL DOOR HEADER

1. Mark the height of the jack stud on each king stud. The height of a jack stud for a standard door is 83½", or ½" taller than the door unit.
2. Cut the 2 × 4 header to span between the king studs at the header marking.
3. Endnail the header to the king stud above the mark for the jack studs.

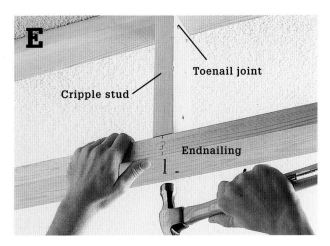

Toenail joint

Cripple stud

Endnailing

After you toenail a cripple stud between the king studs, endnail through the bottom of the header into the cripple stud.

E. INSTALL CRIPPLE STUD FOR DOOR

Install a cripple stud above the header, so it coincides with the 16" stud spacing of the general stud layout. Toenail the cripple stud to the top plate, and endnail through the bottom of the header into the cripple stud.

F. INSTALL JACK STUD FOR DOOR

1. Position the jack studs against the insides of the king studs. Endnail through the top of the header down into the jack studs.
2. Arrange to have any wiring completed by a licensed electrician.

G. CUT WALLBOARD

1. Position the wallboard with the short arm of a T-square flush against the edge.
2. Use a utility knife to score the wallboard face paper along the arm of the square at the desired length.
3. Bend the scored section with both hands to break the plaster core of the wallboard. Fold back unwanted piece and cut through the back paper to separate pieces.

King stud

Jack stud

Header

Endnail through the top of the header down into the jack studs.

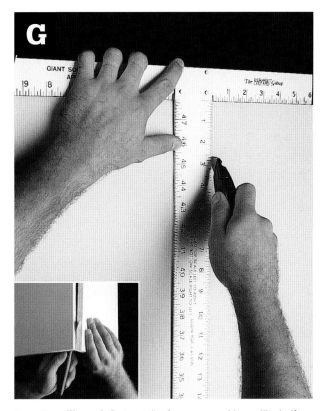

To cut wallboard, first cut the face paper with a utility knife, then snap it back and (inset) finish cut.

Tip ▸

For circular cuts—for working around light fixtures or fans—use an adjustable circle cutter. Mark a center point and use the circle cutter to score both sides of the wallboard. Tap the cut out with a hammer to release it from the surrounding panel.

Lift panels tight against the ceiling with a wallboard lifter, then screw them into position once they are plumb.

Apply a thin layer of wallboard compound over the joint with a 4 or 6" wallboard knife.

To finish inside corners, position the end of a folded tape strip at the top of the joint and press the tape into the wet compound with a wallboard knife.

Tip ▶

Use premixed wallboard compound for most tapping and finishing jobs to eliminate mixing. Use paper wallboard tape when using premixed wallboard compound.

H. INSTALL WALLBOARD

1. Install wallboard, using $\frac{1}{2}$" wallboard for most applications. Plan the wallboard placement so joints do not fall at the corners of doors. Wallboard joints at corners often crack and cause bulges that interfere with miter joints in door trim.
2. Unless the panels are long enough to span the wall, install them vertically to avoid butt joints that are difficult to finish. Plumb the first panel with a level, making sure it breaks on the center of a stud. Lift panels tight against ceiling with a wallboard lifter, and then screw them into position.
3. Anchor wallboard panels by driving $1\frac{1}{4}$" wallboard screws, spaced every 10", into the framing members. Screw heads should be sunk just below the wallboard surface, but should not tear the paper.
4. Add 1× or 2× backing in situations where additional support is necessary to support wallboard edges.

I. TAPE & FINISH WALLBOARD JOINTS

1. Apply a thin layer of wallboard compound over the joint with a 4 or 6" wallboard knife. To load the knife, dip it into a pan filled with wallboard compound.
2. Press the wallboard tape into the compound immediately, centering the tape on the joint. Wipe away the excess compound and smooth the joint with a 6" knife. Let the compound dry overnight.
3. Apply a thin finish coat of compound with a 10" wallboard knife. Allow the second coat to dry and shrink overnight. Apply a final coat and let it dry completely before sanding.

J. FINISH CORNERS

1. To finish inside corners, fold a strip of paper wallboard tape in half by pinching the strip and pulling it between thumb and forefinger. Apply a thin layer of wallboard compound to both sides of the inside corner, using a 4" wallboard knife.
2. Position the end of the folded tape strip at the top of the joint and press the tape into the wet compound with the knife. Smooth both sides of the corner. To finish, see step 3 of Tape & Finish Wallboard Joints (above). *Note: Most walk-in closets have a prehung door, which comes complete with jambs. Now is the time to cut and install the door casings and stain or paint the trim pieces as desired. See page 114 for detailed instructions on door installations.*

New Closets: Building a Reach-in Closet

Many people feel they have a lack of closet space. If you have the space, building a new closet could be the solution to your storage woes.

Whenever possible, position the walls of your closet so they can be anchored to ceiling joists and wall studs. Maintain a minimum depth of 30". Install all needed electrical and plumbing lines in the walls of the closet before hanging the wallboard. Make sure you comply with local building codes when building a closet. Many codes require a permanent light fixture in closets.

The plan shown here presumes a room with 8-ft. ceilings and a closet with a 32" door. If you alter the dimensions, then the sizes of the pieces also will change. Choose the style and size of the door for your closet before you begin the framing. The type of door you choose will determine the size of the rough opening.

Tools, Materials & Cutting List ▸

Stud finder
Framing square
Circular saw
Screw gun or drill
  with bits
Plumb bob
Chalk line
Hammer
Wallboard knives
Wallboard lifter
Level
Tape measure
Ladder
Hand saw

Shims
Corner bead
Nail set
(17) 2 × 4" × 8' pine studs
10d and 16d common nails
8d casing nails
1¼" wallboard nails or screws
Wallboard tape
Wallboard compound
(6) ½" × 4 × 8' wallboard
32 × 80" prehung interior
  door kit
Finishing materials

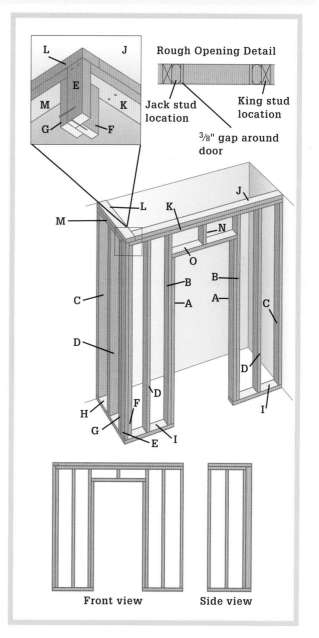

Rough Opening Detail

Jack stud location

King stud location

⅜" gap around door

Front view

Side view

Key	Part	Dimension	Pcs.
A	Jack stud	1½ × 3½ × 83½"	2
B	King stud	1½ × 3½ × 91½"	2
C	End stud	1½ × 3½ × 91½"	2
D	Intermediate stud	1½ × 3½ × 91½"	3
E	Outside corner stud	1½ × 3½ × 93"	1
F	Inside corner stud	1½ × 3½ × 91½"	1
G	Corner stud	1½ × 3½ × 91½"	1
H	Side wall sole plate	1½ × 3½ × 31½"	1
I	Front wall sole plate	1½ × 3½ × 30"	2
J	Upper top plate, front wall	1½ × 3½ × 90½"	1
K	Lower top plate, front wall	1½ × 3½ × 92½"	1
L	Upper top plate, side wall	1½ × 3½ × 35"	1
M	Lower top plate, side wall	1½ × 3½ × 31½"	1
N	Cripple stud	1½ × 3½ × 6½"	1
O	Header	1½ × 3½ × 37"	1

How to Build a Reach-in Closet

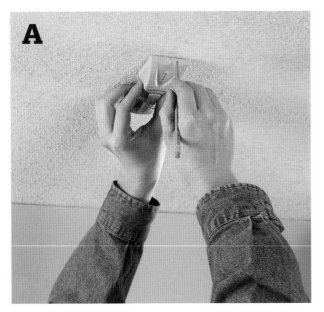

A

Locate the existing wall studs and ceiling joists. Mark the direction and edges of each joist with a pencil.

B

Check the pencil line with a framing square to ensure the layout is correctly placed.

Tip ▶

If the top plates for one of the new walls cannot be anchored to a ceiling joist, start the top plate installation with the plates that can be anchored.

1. Measure and cut the upper and lower top plates for the wall that can be anchored to the ceiling joists. Position the upper top plate flush with the lines on the ceiling and drive 16d nails through the top plate into the ceiling joists.
2. Attach the lower top plate to the upper top plate with 10d nails, making sure the side edges of the two plates are flush, and the ends are spaced properly for the corner construction.
3. Measure and cut the top plates for the remaining wall to length. Facenail the two plates together with 10d nails, making sure the side edges are flush.
4. Position the top plate assembly on the ceiling layout and drive 16d nails through the lower top plate of the front wall into the upper top plate of the side wall. Attach the other end of the top plates by toenailing 16d nails through the top plate assembly, into the top plate of the existing wall.

A. LOCATE STUDS & JOISTS

1. Use a stud finder to locate the wall studs and ceiling joists in the planned closet location.
2. Locate the edges of each framing member and mark the direction of the ceiling joists.

B. LAY OUT THE TOP PLATE LOCATIONS

1. Whenever possible, adjust dimensions to line up with ceiling joists and wall studs. The double top plate construction makes it possible to build the closet even if the top plates for one of the walls cannot be attached to a ceiling joist, but the end studs for each wall must be fastened to the studs or top and sole plates in the existing walls.
2. Measure out from the back and side walls and make reference marks for the locations of new top plates.
3. Use a framing square to make sure the reference marks are straight and perpendicular to the back wall.
4. Using a laser level, join the reference marks with a pencil line. Use a framing square to ensure lines are straight and perpendicular with existing walls.

Install the side wall top plates with 16d nails driven into the ceiling joists.

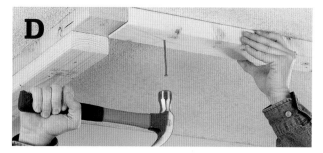

Facenail the front wall top plates with 16d nails.

Take multiple plumb bob readings to determine the locations of the sole plates.

C. INSTALL TOP PLATES FOR SIDE WALL

1. Measure and cut upper and lower top plates for the side wall. The lower top plate should be $3\frac{1}{2}$" shorter than the upper top plate to allow space for the corner construction. Position the upper top plate of the side wall flush with the pencil lines and drive 16d nails through the top plate into the ceiling joists.
2. Attach the lower top plate to the upper top plate with 10d nails, making sure the side edges of the top plates are flush and the spacing is accurate for the corner construction.

D. INSTALL TOP PLATES FOR FRONT WALL

1. Cut upper and lower top plates for the front wall to length with a circular saw. Make sure the lower top plate is 2" longer than the upper top plate to allow space for the corner construction. Position the upper top plate of the front wall flush with the pencil lines and facenail it to the ceiling joists with 16d nails.
2. Position the lower top plate against the upper top plate so the side edges are flush and the spacing is accurate for the corner construction. Facenail the lower top plate to the upper top plate with 10d nails.

E. LAY OUT THE ROUGH OPENING & SOLE PLATES

1. Measure and mark the layout for rough opening framing members of the door on the lower top plate of the front wall. The width of the rough opening should equal the width of the door frame plus $\frac{3}{8}$" on each side. Make marks indicating the jack and king stud locations.
2. Determine the position of the sole plates with multiple plumb bob readings. Hang a plumb bob from the outside edges of each end of the top plate assemblies for both new walls. The tip of the plumb bob should nearly touch the floor. When it is completely motionless, mark the plumb bob's position on the floor with a pencil.
3. Take additional plumb bob readings from the door-side mark of both jack studs to indicate the end of each bottom plate for the front wall.
4. Snap chalk lines on the floor, marking the locations for sole plates. Then use a right angle square to square off the ends of the markings for the sole plates of the front wall, indicating the beginning of the rough opening for the door.

Install the sole plates with 10d nails driven every 16".

Toenail the end and intermediate studs with 10d nails driven into the lower top plates and the sole plates.

Fasten the corner stud assembly with 10d nails. Follow the Corner Detail drawing on page 97.

Endnail the header flush with the reference marks indicating the height of the jack studs.

F. INSTALL THE SOLE PLATES

Measure and cut the sole plates to length. Following the chalk lines snapped on the floor, install the sole plates with 10d nails driven through the sole plates at 16" intervals. Make sure the plates are flush with the chalk lines.

G. INSTALL THE END AND INTERMEDIATE STUDS

1. Measure and cut the end studs to length.
2. Toenail the end studs to the top and sole plates with 10d nails. Facenail the end studs to the existing wall studs with 16d nails.
3. Measure and cut the intermediate studs to length individually, working from the existing walls toward the new corner. Install the studs at intervals no greater than 24" so the wallboard will have proper backing. Toenail the studs to the lower top plates and sole plates with 10d nails.

H. INSTALL THE CORNER ASSEMBLY

Refer to the Corner Assembly Detail on page 97 for the exact placement of studs and the nailing method of the corner assembly.

1. Measure and cut the three studs of the corner assembly to length.
2. Toenail and endnail each stud to the top and sole plates with 10d nails. Then drive 10d nails through the surface of each stud as shown in the Corner Detail.

I. INSTALL THE KING STUDS & HEADER

1. Measure, cut, and toenail the king studs with 10d nails on the king stud markings of the lower top plate and 1½" from the end of each sole plate.
2. Use a combination square and a pencil to mark the height of the jack stud on each king stud. The height of a jack stud for a standard door is 83½", or ½" taller than the door.
3. Cut the header to fit snugly between the king studs and endnail it to the king studs so the bottom edge is flush with the reference lines indicating the height of the jack studs.

Drive 10d nails through the top of the header into the ends of the jack studs.

Install wallboard panels using a screwgun and 1¼" wallboard screws, spacing the screws every 10".

Apply wallboard compound to joints with a 6" wallboard knife, and then press wallboard tape into the compound. Smooth tape with the knife. For corners (inset), install corner bead with nails or screws driven every 8".

Tip ▶

Plan the layout of the wallboard panels, avoiding joints that fall at the corners of the door opening. Joints at these corners often crack and cause bulges that interfere with door trim installation. Unless the panels span the entire wall, install them vertically to avoid butt joints that are difficult to finish.

J. INSTALL THE JACK & CRIPPLE STUDS

1. Measure, cut, and position the jack studs against the inside surface of the king studs, making sure the edges are flush. Endnail the jack studs in place, driving 10d nails through the header, into the jack.
2. Measure and cut a header cripple stud to coincide with the general stud layout.
3. Toenail the cripple stud to the lower top plate, and drive 10d nails through the bottom of the header into the cripple stud.

K. HANG THE WALLBOARD

1. Install any electrical wiring in the walls before you begin to hang the wallboard.
2. Hang wallboard on the interior and exterior of the closet, beginning with the interior. Use a wallboard lifter to raise the panels tight against the ceiling. Measure and cut each panel to size, working from one end of the closet to the other (see page 95 for help with cutting wallboard). Plumb the first panel with a level, making sure the side edges fall on the center of a stud and are flush with the existing wall. Attach each panel with 1¼" wallboard screws driven every 10" into the studs.

L. FINISH THE WALLBOARD JOINTS

1. Apply a thin layer of wallboard compound over the joints with a 4 or 6" wallboard knife. Press wallboard tape into the compound immediately, centering the tape on the joint. Wipe away any excess compound and smooth the joint with a 6" knife. Let the compound dry overnight.
2. Apply a thin finish coat of compound with a 10" wallboard knife. Allow the second coat to dry and shrink overnight.
3. Apply the last coat and let it dry before sanding the joints smooth.
4. To finish inside corners, see page 96.
5. Position corner bead on the outside corner. Use a level to adjust the bead so the corner is plumb and attach it with 1¼" wallboard nails or screws spaced at 8" intervals.
6. Cover the corner bead with three coats of wallboard compound, using a 6 or 10" wallboard knife. *Note: To install the prehung interior door and door casing, see page 117.*

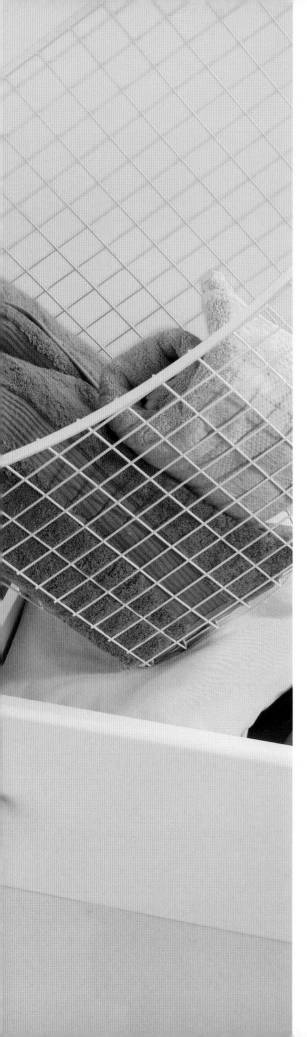

Adding Accessories

Once you have your closet system in place, accessories add the final touch. These items accent any closet and are often credited for the luxury and personal touch associated with custom closets. In this section several of the most popular custom accessories are explained in detail to allow you to put them to use with ease.

In this section:
- Rods
- Shoe Cubby
- Tie & Belt Rack
- Drawers
- Cabinet Doors
- Closet Doors
- Ventilation Systems
- Baskets
- Vertical Spacers
- Closet Island
- Drawer Components

Rods

Rod end caps can be bought with 32mm pins to fit in the shelf-pin holes on the vertical panels. These are easily adjustable. There are also manufacturer rods that you must screw into the vertical panels.

Small plastic rods

Metal or stainless steel rods

Wood dowels

Painted wood dowels

How to Cut Rods to Size

Closet rods come in a variety of styles—including wood, steel, and plastic—and sizes. If needed, you can cut rods to size. Be sure to buy rod end caps to fit the diameter of the rod you choose.

A. MEASURE BETWEEN VERTICALS
1. Clamp the end caps to the verticals according to the manufacturer instructions.
2. Measure between the two end caps to determine the length needed for the rod. Remember to allow for the manufacturer end cap as well (typically ¼").
3. Mark the cutline on your rod.

B. CUT ROD TO SIZE
1. Fasten the rod into a jig or onto a workbench for safety.
2. Use a hacksaw to cut custom metal rod sizes.

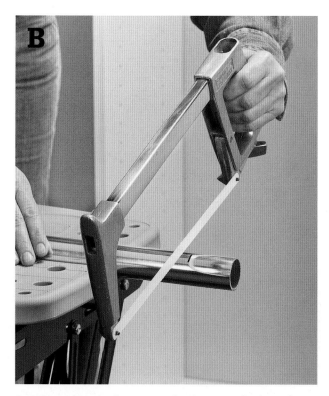

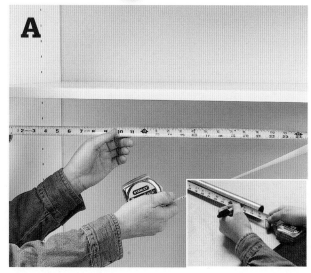

If your custom design doesn't match manufacturer rod sizes, measure the interior space in between the two vertical end caps, then mark this cutline on your rod.

Cut the rod to size for your application. Use a hacksaw for metal rods and circular saw for wood rods.

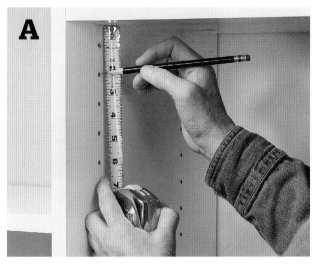

Measure 1½" down from the underside of top shelf to allow for adequate hanger clearance.

Align the end cap on center to a shelf-pin hole and press manufacturer pins through the cap hole to fasten cap to vertical.

How to Add Closet Rods

A. MARK END CAP LOCATIONS

1. Measure down 1½" from the underside of the top shelf and make a mark on the vertical for hanger clearance.
2. Repeat for the other vertical that will support the rod.

B. FASTEN END CAPS TO VERTICALS

1. Center the rod end over the marks and on center with the shelf-pin holes on the vertical.
2. Insert rod end caps into shelf-pin holes according to manufacturer instructions.

C. PLACE ROD

1. Lower the rod into place. Be sure the rod snaps securely into place.
2. Check for level and adjust as necessary.

ALTERNATIVE: USING SCREW-MOUNTED END CAPS

1. Measure down 1½" and make a mark for hanger clearance. Repeat for the other vertical that will support the rod.
2. Center the rod end cap over the mark and on center with the shelf-pin holes on the vertical.
3. Hold the rod end cap in place over marks and drill manufacturer screws through end cap holes and into vertical panel. Repeat for the other side.

Hold the rod over each end cap and lower into place.

Alternative: Use the predrilled holes at locations for screw-mounted end caps as well.

Shoe Cubby

This shoe cubby is designed to slide on top of a shelf in an existing unit (as shown on page 44). The vertical spacers are fixed to the top shelf, and all other shelving is adjustable. To ensure your cubby pars align with the verticals in the section the cubby will reside, it's crucial to have the entire custom closet unit level and plumb before attempting to cut cubby parts.

Tools, Materials & Cutting List ▸

Measuring tape
Circular saw with
    melamine blade
Framing square
Drill
20mm bits
Rubber mallet

2" wood screws
Caps for screw holes
Screwdriver
(36) shelf pins
(2) KDs with screws
(2) KDs with screw/
    dowels

Key	Part	Dimension	Pcs.	Material
A	Cubby pars	24 × 12 × 18 ½"	2	¾" melamine shelf stock with predrilled pin holes
B	Fixed shelf	24 × 12"	1	¾" melamine shelf stock with predrilled pin holes
C	Adjustable shelves	7¾ × 12"	9	½" melamine

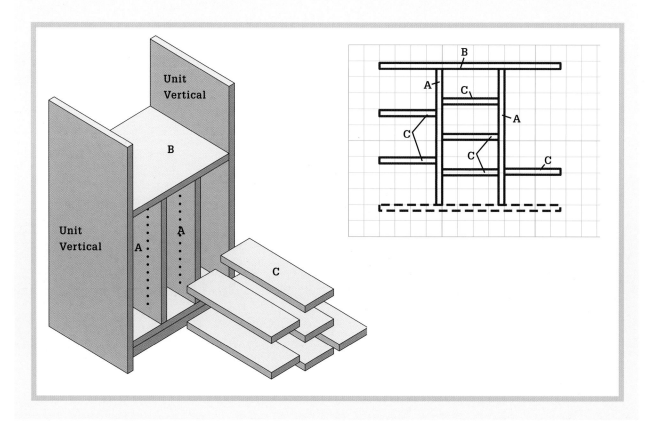

How to Build a Custom Shoe Cubby

A. PREPARE PARS

1. Level and plumb the entire custom closet unit.
2. In the section the cubby will reside, measure from the bottom shelf (which the cubby will sit on) up to the first shelf-pin hole of a vertical (left and right vertical pin holes in this section should match if unit is level). Be sure to measure to the center of the hole.
3. Transfer the measurement taken in step 2 to your first shoe cubby par (make sure the par is the same depth as the custom closet unit—here it is 12"). Measure from the bottom of predrilled shelf stock up to the nearest shelf-pin hole. If the measurement doesn't align on center with a predrilled pin hole, move up to the nearest hole on center and measure down to create a new base cutline. Cut shelf stock at this mark using a circular saw with a melamine blade. *Note: If you are drilling your own pin holes, simply measure up from the melamine bottom edge and make a mark for your first pin hole center. Follow the instructions on page 46 for drilling the pin holes.*

4. From the base cutline, measure up $18\frac{1}{2}$" and make a mark. Cut the shelf at this mark using a circular saw with a melamine blade.
5. Repeat steps 2 through 4 for the other cubby par.

B. CUT FIXED SHELF

1. On $\frac{3}{4}$"-thick melamine shelf stock with predrilled holes mark the length at $23\frac{1}{4}$". Using a framing square, draw a line across the shelf stock at mark.
2. Cut the shelf at cutline, using a circular saw with a melamine blade.

C. PREPARE FIXED SHELF

1. Mark the final placement location for KDs (on center to shelf-pin holes on verticals). Set the KDs back from shelf edges based on size, following manufacturer instructions (see page 46 for help with marking and drilling holes for KDs).
2. Drill a hole on fixed shelf for KDs, using a bit size recommended by the manufacturer (20mm is standard). Mark the stop location on your bit with tape so you don't drill through the board.
3. Tap KDs into place on fixed shelves using a rubber mallet.

Measure from the bottom shelf, which the cubby will rest upon, up to the desired height. Align height mark on center to shelf-pin hole (inset).

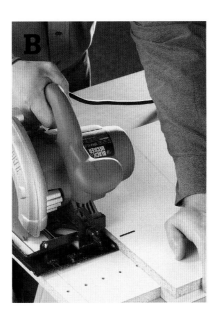

Cut the top shelf with a circular saw with a melamine blade.

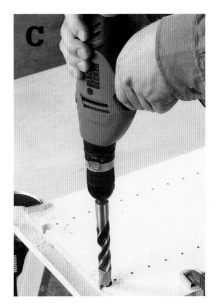

Align the fixed shelves with pars and mark for KD on underside of shelves.

Countersink screws through the fixed shelf into pars.

When measuring the cuts for shelving, be sure to compensate for cut waste based on your type of circular saw blade.

D. ATTACH FIXED SHELF TO VERTICALS

1. Measure in 7¾" from the left (vertical) side of the fixed shelf and make two marks 3" in from the front and back edges on the underside of the shelf. This is the center placement for the pars.
2. Drill a pilot hole at marks.
3. Set a par on center to marks on fixed shelf. Countersink 2" screws through the top of the fixed shelf down into the center of the par at marks.
4. Repeat steps 1 and 2 for the other par on the right side.
5. Place a cap in the countersunk holes for a smooth finish.

E. PREPARE ADJUSTABLE SHELVES

1. Measure out nine 12 × 7" shelves on a piece of ½"-thick melamine shelf stock without predrilled holes.
2. Cut the shelf stock at cutlines, using a circular saw with a melamine blade.

F. FINISH

1. Set the shoe cubby unit in place within your custom closet.
2. Lock down cams on the fixed shelf, using a screwdriver. The left side has a cam and screw, while the right side has a cam and dowel (which fits over the screw on the other side of the vertical that is attached to another fixed shelf—see plans on page 44).
3. Add shelf pins where desired and slide in adjustable shelving.

It is easiest to install adjustable shelving by first tilting it at a 45° angle, sliding it into place, and then lowering it down level onto the shelf pegs. Tap into place, if necessary.

Ties & Belt Rack

There are several tie and belt racks for sale. The manufacturer versions are often made to attach directly into the shelf pin holes on the verticals in your custom closet, making placement and adjustability a breeze. You can find those racks at home centers and online (see Resources on page 140). To make a custom tie and belt rack, follow the instructions given here. This heavy-duty cedar hanger will protect your winter coats from moth damage when used as a standard hanger, or it can keep your ties and belts organized and easily accessible.

This manufacturer tie rack fastens directly into predrilled shelf-pin holes. Such versions are widely available and easy to install.

Tools, Materials & Cutting List ▶

Drill with bits
Jigsaw
Sander with 120-grit sandpaper
Combination square

Key	Part	Dimension	Pcs.
A	Hanger body*	1 × 6 × 20"	1
B	Shoulder hooks	1¼"	13
C	Cup hooks	⁵⁄₁₆"	8
D	Large utility hook		1

*Material: aromatic cedar

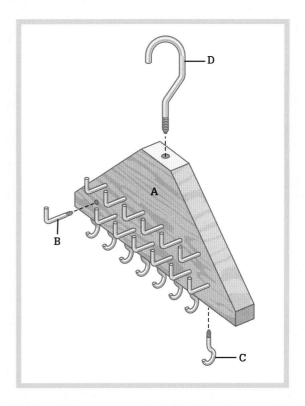

How to Make a Tie & Belt Rack

A. MAKE THE HANGER BODY

1. Trace the outline of the body of a standard plastic or metal hanger onto a piece of 1" aromatic cedar. Use a jigsaw to cut along the outline.
2. Sand the hanger body, using 120-grit sandpaper. Round edges and smooth faces.

B. LAY OUT THE BELT HOOK LOCATIONS

1. Mark a center line across the face of the workpiece using a combination square. Extend the line across the bottom and top edges.
2. To make the layout for the belt hooks, measure 2" on either side of the center-line mark and draw reference marks across the bottom edge of the workpiece. Measuring toward the outside edges from your reference marks, draw additional marks in 1½" increments for each belt hook.
3. Set a combination square to half the thickness of the hanger, and use the end of the ruler as a guide to draw reference X marks through the previous marks for each belt hook location.

C. LAY OUT TIE & HANGING HOOK LOCATIONS

1. Position one edge of a combination square ruler flush with the lower edge of the workpiece so the end of the ruler is flush with the center line. Draw a horizontal line 1" from the bottom edge, then without moving the ruler make a vertical reference mark 1" from the center line. Make additional reference marks in 1½" increments toward the outer edge for as many hooks as desired.
2. Make an additional horizontal reference line 1" above the first line and repeat the previous step. To stagger the layout of the tie hooks, the first mark should be ¾" from the center mark and in 1½" increments to the outer edge.
3. Repeat the steps taken to lay out the hook locations on the other side of the center line, and the back of the workpiece, if desired.
4. To find the large utility hook location on the top of the workpiece, set the combination square ruler to half the thickness of the workpiece. Position the square flush with the front side of the workpiece and make a reference line through the center line across the top edge.
5. Drill ¼"-deep pilot holes at every reference mark for a tie or belt hook. Drill a ½"-deep pilot hole for the utility hook at the intersection of the two reference lines on the top edge of the hanger.
6. Erase all reference marks and screw the shoulder hooks in the tie holes and the cup hooks in the belt holes. Finally, screw the utility hook in place. Do not apply finish. Sand the hanger on occasion with fine sandpaper to replenish the scent.

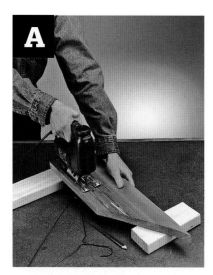

Cut the aromatic cedar with even pressure applied to the saw, or your cuts will be rough and more difficult to sand.

Use a combination square to make straight, accurate reference marks.

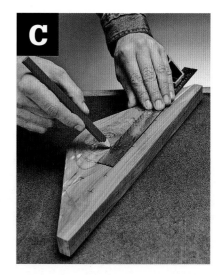

Offset the reference marks in the second tier of tie hooks by measuring out ¾" from the center mark.

Drawers

The melamine drawers sold at home centers will work for the modular installations in this book. It is a good idea to find out which sizes are available before designing the size of the section in which the drawers will be placed. Standard sizes include 16 × 10", 25 × 5", and 25 × 10".

To make your own custom drawers to fit any sized section (with an average maximum of 36"), adjust the parts sizes and then follow the simple instructions in this project. Be sure to use glue specifically for melamine products when making drawers out of melamine—regular wood glue does not work as well.

Tools, Materials & Cutting List ▸

Circular saw with a melamine blade
Biscuit joiner
Drill and ³⁄₁₆" bit
Piloting bit for screws
Iron
1¼" and 1½" deck screws
Tack-on drawer glides
Melamine glue
Biscuits
Heat-activated veneer tape
Other finishing materials (as desired)

Key	Part	Dimension	Pcs.
A	Drawer sides	¾ × 3½ × 10¾"	2
B	Drawer ends	3½ × 12½ × ¾"	2
C	Drawer front	5 × 15¾" × ¾"	1
D	Drawer bottom	9 × 12½ × ¾"	1

Note: Measurements reflect the actual size of dimension lumber. Custom sizes must be made to fit custom sections in which drawers will be placed.

How to Build Drawers

A. BUILD THE DRAWER

1. Cut drawer bottom, front, ends, and sides to size using a circular saw with a melamine blade.
2. Lay out the two mating pieces of material on a flat surface. Draw a line midway across the joint. Position the drawer bottom between the ends, keeping the bottom edges and the ends flush. Mark two locations near the center along a drawer end's side. Mark the same locations on the drawer bottom's side. This is the center line for the biscuits. Hold a biscuit centered over the spaces to be sure they are spaced at least 4" apart.
3. Align the drawer sides so their front edges are flush with the front face of the front drawer end. Repeat step 2 through 4 for the drawer sides.
4. At marks, use a biscuit joiner to cut slots for the biscuits. Test-fit biscuits in the slots and align drawer ends and sides with drawer bottom.
5. Cover the slots on each drawer end with glue, and insert the biscuits. Insert glue into bottom unit slots, and then fit the slots together.
6. Position the drawer bottom between the ends, keeping the bottom edges and ends flush. *Note: Biscuits swell once they are in contact with glue.*
7. Countersink 1½" drywall screws through the drawer ends and into the drawer bottom at each corner. Repeat for drawer sides.
8. Fasten sides to ends with 1½" countersunk drywall screws. Rear ends of drawer sides overhang the rear drawer end by ¼".
9. Draw a reference line along the inside face of the drawer front ¼" above the bottom edge. Lay the front flat. Center the drawer from side to side on the front with its bottom edge on the reference line. Apply glue, and drive 1¼" drywall screws through the drawer end and into the front.

B. INSTALL GLIDE ONTO VERTICALS & ADD DRAWER KNOBS

1. Fasten the glide to verticals with panhead screws. *Note: For verticals with predrilled shelf-pin holes some manufacturers of drawer glides suggest to insert Euro or barrel screws through glide and into predrilled holes.*
2. Fasten the drawer knobs to the drawer front. Be sure to space the knobs evenly, and center them from top to bottom on the drawer front.
3. Fill all countersunk screw holes with plastic caps, add edge tape to exposed edges (see page 47).

C. INSTALL THE HARDWARE

Store-bought kits include all of the hardware needed to install a track system. Always follow manufacturer directions when installing hardware.

1. Align the glides along the path of the drawer so they line up with track on vertical.
2. Fasten glides to drawers with panhead screws.
3. Insert the drawer. With the drawer open slightly, reach in and rotate the drawer stop until it is in position to catch the stop cleat.

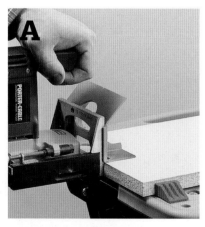

Make biscuit slots with a biscuit joiner. Fasten the drawer sides and ends to the drawer bottom with melamine glue and biscuits. Reinforce with screws.

Fasten glides to verticals at predrilled holes with Euro or barrel screws.

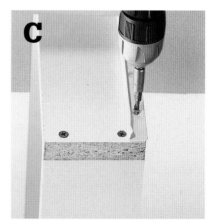

Install drawer glides along the path of the drawer according to manufacturer instructions.

Cabinet Doors

Cabinet doors are easy to make using ½" finish-grade plywood and door-edge moldings. The ½" finish-grade veneer material at most home centers—in oak, maple, or birch—tends to warp and won't stay flat unless it's attached to a rigid hardwid form. The ¾" finish-grade stays flatter than ½", but it can be a little bulky for doors. Cabinet-grade plywood is a big step up in quality. Also called "hardwood-core," this plywood is made stiffer and stronger than standard (veneer-core) plywood mentioned above, and it's less likely to warp.

Measure the width and height of the door opening from the outer edge of verticals and fixed shelves.

Attach hinges to the verticals and door. Then attach door according to manufacturer instructions.

Attach door handles or knobs, and any door catch hardware.

How to Build & Install Cabinet Doors without Face Frames

A. PREPARE DOOR
Measure the width and height of the door opening from the outer edge of verticals and fixed shelves. Cut one or two door panels from ¾" melamine. For one door, the door panel should equal the width and height of the door opening plus the surrounding verticals and fixed shelves (each ¾" thick). For two doors, each door panel should equal this same measured height of the opening. The width of each panel will be half the total width of the opening, minus ½". For example: if opening is 14" high × 36" wide, each door panel should be 14" high × 17½" wide. *Tip: If the opening is wider than 24", two doors are necessary.*

B. MOUNT HINGES TO DOOR
1. Mount two fully concealed overlay hinges (cup or Euro hinges) to the back of the door, 2" from the top and bottom. *Note: Use three hinges if the door is taller than 30".*
2. Attach the other half of the hinges to the verticals, following the hinge manufacturer instructions.

C. ATTACH HANDLES
Attach door handles or knobs, and any door catch hardware, following manufacturer directions.

Alternative: How to Build & Install an Overlay Cabinet Door with Face Frames

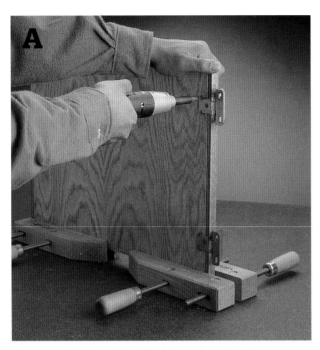

Mount two semi-concealed overlay hinges to the back of the door, 2" from the top and bottom.

A. MOUNT HINGES TO DOOR

1. Measure the width and height of the door opening. Cut one or two door panels from ½" finish-grade plywood. For one door, the door panel should equal the width and height of the door opening. For two doors, each door panel should equal the measured height of the opening. The width of each panel will be half the total width of the opening, minus ½". For example: if opening is 14" high × 36" wide, each door panel should be 14" high × 17½" wide. *Tip: If the opening is wider than 24", two doors are necessary.*

2. For each door, measure and cut door-edge molding to frame the door panel, mitering the ends at a 45° angle.

3. Attach door-edge molding to door panel by drilling pilot holes and driving 1½" finish nails through the side of the molding and into the door panels. Finish the door to match the built-in.

4. Mount two semi-concealed overlay hinges to the back of the door, 2" from the top and bottom. *Note: Use three hinges if the door is taller than 30".*

Open the hinges and position the door over the opening so it is aligned with the tape reference marks. Drill pilot holes and anchor the hinges to the face frame with mounting screws.

Attach door knobs or handles, following manufacturer instructions.

B. MOUNT DOOR TO FACE FRAME

1. Use masking tape to mark a reference line on the top face frame rail, ½" above the door opening.

2. Position the door over the opening, aligning the top edge with the tape reference line. Mark one hinge location on the face frame with masking tape.

3. Open the hinges, and position the door against the edge of the face frame so the hinge is aligned with the tape marking the hinge locations. Drill pilot holes, and anchor the hinges to the face frame with the mounting screws. Remove the masking tape.

C. ATTACH HANDLES

Attach door handles or knobs, and any door catch hardware, following manufacturer directions.

Closet Doors

Choosing the right door requires some thought and evaluation. A door should complement the architectural style of a home—or the design of the room in which it resides—as well as meet the specific needs of its location. The door you choose for your closet can significantly enhance the look and feel of a room.

Closet doors, for example, largely offer privacy. But if you prefer an open, contemporary feel to a room, you may want to create an illusion of openness by choosing translucent or colored glass doors. If you worked really hard at customizing your closet, you may want to showcase it with clear glass doors!

When planning your project, keep in mind that interior passage doors into a walk-in closet must be at least 30" wide, and they are usually 1⅜" thick. However, for greater accessibility, all interior doors should be a minimum of 32" wide. Double-entry doors, such as French style doors, may be 60, 64, or 72" wide. The standard height for any door is 80".

The material you choose is just as important as the style. Closet doors may be hollow-core or solid-core. French doors incorporate glass panels in their design.

The basic steps for framing a rough opening for an interior prehung door are the same for closet doors. However, for large closet openings, such as for double bifold or bypass doors, use a built-up header: two 2 × 4s set on edge and nailed together with a strip of ½"-thick plywood in between. This provides additional strength to support the weight of the doors.

Most bifold doors are designed to fit in an 80"-high finished opening. Wood bifold doors have the advantage of allowing you to trim doors to fit openings that are slightly shorter.

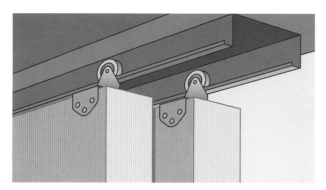

Standard bypass door openings are 4, 5, 6, or 8'. The finished width should be 1" narrower than the combined width of the doors to provide a 1" overlap when the doors are closed. For long closets that require three or more doors, subtract another 1" from the width of the finished opening for each door. Check the hardware installation instructions for the required height of the opening.

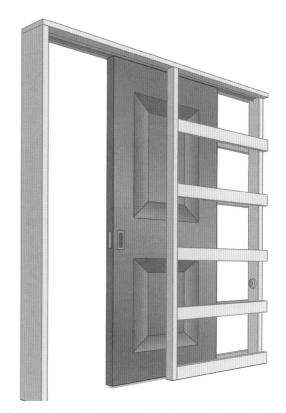

The rough opening for a pocket door must be roughly twice the width of the door itself to allow the door to slide completely into the enclosure in the finished wall. The enclosure is formed by nailing a pocket door cage (available at home centers) to the framing, then adding wallboard and trim. Consult the cage manufacturer's instructions for the dimensions of the rough opening.

Door Openings ▸

The projects that follow show you how to build door frames and install new doors for your closets. First you must identify if your wall is load-bearing. Load-bearing walls carry the structural weight of your home. In platform-frame houses, load-bearing walls can be identified by double top plates made from two layers of framing lumber. Load-bearing walls included all exterior walls and any interior walls that are aligned above support beams. If you discover the wall is load-bearing, consult a building professional to discuss your project.

Nonload-bearing, or partition, walls are interior walls that do not carry the structural weight of the house. They have a single top plate and can be perpendicular to floor and ceiling joists but are not aligned above support beams. Any interior wall that is parallel to floor and ceiling joists is a partition wall.

Although different door styles require different frame openings, the same basic framing techniques are used. Purchase the doors and hardware in advance, and consult the hardware manufacturer's instructions for exact dimensions of the rough opening for the type of door you select.

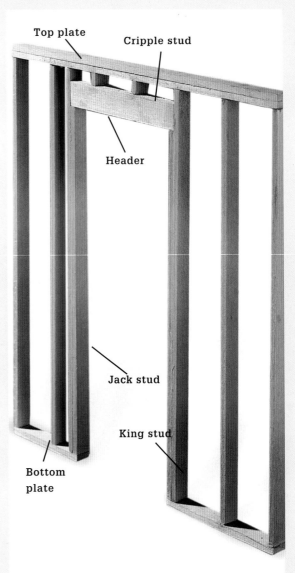

Built-up Header

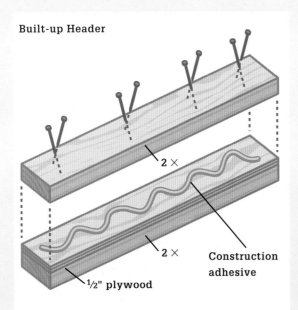

Door frames have king studs attached to the wall plates and jack studs that support the header. Cripple studs transfer the load from above onto the header and are placed to maintain the stud layout. The dimensions of the framed opening are called the rough opening.

Door frames, called rough openings, are sized according to the dimensions of the door unit. In load-bearing walls, the weight from above the opening is borne by the cripple studs, which are supported by a header that spans the opening. A typical header is made with two pieces of two 2 × 4s or 2 × 6s set on edge and glued and nailed together with a strip of ½"-thick plywood in between (see illustration). This creates a rigid horizontal member to help support the weight of the doors, which is necessary for large closet openings with heavy, double bifold or bypass doors. Some builders use oversized headers, which eliminate the need for cripples. Frames in nonload-bearing walls may have only a single 2 × 4 for a header. Each end of the header is supported by a jack stud that extends to the bottom plate and is nailed to a king stud for support.

Prehung Doors

Prehung doors come as single units with the door already hung on hinges attached to a factory-built frame. To secure the unit during shipping, most prehung doors are braced or nailed shut with a couple of duplex nails driven through the jambs and into the door edge. These nails must be removed before you install the door. The key to installing doors is to plumb and fasten the hinge-side jamb first. After that's in place, you can position the top and latch-side jambs by checking the reveal (the gap between the closed door and the jamb).

Standard prehung doors have $4\frac{1}{2}$"-wide jambs and are sized to fit walls with 2×4 construction and $\frac{1}{2}$" wallboard. If you have thicker walls, you can special-order doors to match, or you can add jamb extensions to standard-size doors.

Tools & Materials ▸

Miter saw	4-ft. level	Prehung door unit	4d and 6d finish nails
Straightedge	Nail set	Wood shims	Door casing
Drill and bits	Handsaw	8d casing nails	Wood putty

How to Install a Prehung Door

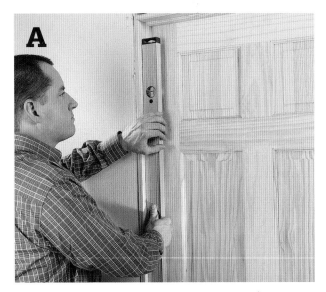

Set the door unit into the framed opening. Using a level, adjust the unit so the hinge-side jamb is plumb.

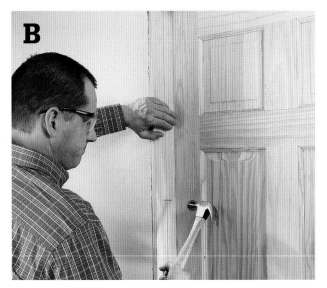

Anchor the hinge-side jamb with 8d casing nails.

A. ALIGN DOOR UNIT

Slide the door unit into the framed opening so the edges of the jambs are flush with the wall surface and the hinge-side jamb is plumb.

B. INSERT DOOR SHIMS

1. Insert pairs of wood shims driven from opposite directions into the space between the framing members and the hinge-side jamb. Check the hinge-side jamb to make sure it is still plumb and does not bow.
2. Anchor the hinge-side jamb with 8d casing nails driven through the jamb and shims and into the jack stud.
3. Insert pairs of shims in the space between the framing members and latch-side jamb and top jamb. With the door closed, adjust the shims so the gap between door edge and jamb is 1/8" wide. Drive 8d casing nails through the jambs and shims, into the framing members.

C. FINISH INSTALLATION

1. Set all nails below the surface of the wood with a nail set.
2. Cut the shims flush with the wall surface, using a handsaw. Hold the saw vertically to prevent damage to the door jamb or wall.
3. Finish the door and install the lockset as directed by the manufacturer.

Cut the shims flush with the wall surface, using a handsaw.

D

Measure the distance between the side casings, and cut the top casing to fit.

D. PREPARE HEAD CASINGS & MARK SIDE CASINGS

1. On each jamb, mark a reveal line ⅛" from the inside edge. The casings will be installed flush with these lines.
2. Cut the head casing to length. Mark the centerpoint of the head casings and the centerpoint of the head jamb. Align the casing with the head jamb reveal line, matching the centerpoints so that the head casing extends evenly beyond both side jambs. Nail the casing to the wall at stud locations and at the jamb.
3. Hold the side casings against the head casing and mark them for cutting.

E. CUT SIDE CASINGS

Cut the side casings to length. *Note: If desired, make 45° miter cuts on the top end of the casing. Measure and cut the other vertical casing piece, using the same method.*

F. FASTEN SIDE CASINGS

Align the side casings with the side jamb reveal lines, and then nail the casings to the jambs and framing members. Set the nails using a nail set. Fill the nail holes with wood putty.

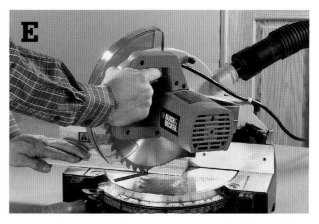

Using a miter saw, make 45° cuts on the ends of the moldings.

Locknail the corner joints by drilling pilot holes and driving 4d finish nails through each corner, as shown.

French Doors

French doors create a grand entrance into a custom closet. They consist of two separate doors hinged on opposing jambs of a doorway. For a closet, you'll most likely want the doors top open into the room, providing easier access to closet items. French doors are typically sold in prehung units.

Before purchasing a prehung French door unit, determine the size of doors you need. If you plan to install the doors in an existing doorway, measure the dimensions of the rough opening (from the unfinished framing members), and then order the unit to size according to manufacturer recommendations.

If you must alter the existing opening (as shown in this project), build the rough opening a little larger than the outside dimensions of the door unit. Prehung units typically require adding 1" to the width and ½" to the height.

If the doorway is in a load-bearing wall, set up temporary supports and install an appropriately sized header. Depth is critical: it's based on the length of the header, the material it's made from, and the weight of the load it must support. For actual requirements, consult your local building department.

Tools & Materials ▸

Tape measure	Prehung French door
Circular saw	unit
Reciprocating saw	2 × 4 lumber
4-ft. level	2 × 6 lumber
Hammer	10d and 16d common
Handsaw	nails
Drill	Wood shims
Utility knife	8d finish nails
Nail set	

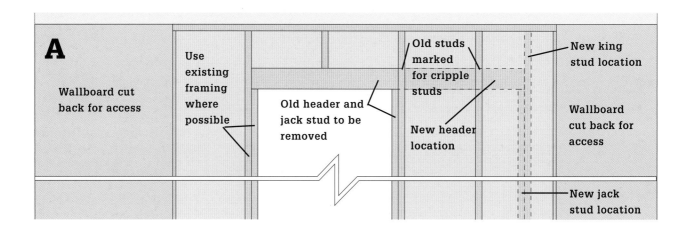

How to Install French Doors

A. FRAME THE ROUGH OPENING

1. Shut off power and water to the area. Remove the wall surfaces from both sides of the wall, leaving one stud bay open on each side of the new rough opening. Also remove or reroute any wiring, plumbing, or ductwork. Lay out the new rough opening, marking the locations of all new jack and king studs on both the top and bottom plates. Where practical, use existing framing members. *Tip: To install a new king stud, cut a stud to size and align with the layout marks, toenail to the bottom plate with 10d common nails, check for plumb, and then toenail to the top plate. Finally, mark both the bottom and top of the new header on one king stud, then use a level to extend the lines across the intermediate studs to the opposite king stud. If using existing framing, measure from the existing jack stud.*

2. Cut the intermediate studs at the reference marks for the top of the header, using a reciprocating saw or handsaw. Pry the studs away from the sole plates and remove. The remaining top pieces will be used as cripple studs.

Holding the prehung door in the framed opening, insert shims into the gap between the framing and the jamb. Check the jamb to make sure it remains plumb.

3. To install a jack stud, cut the stud to fit between the sole plate and the bottom of the header, as marked on the king stud. Align it at the mark against the king stud, and then fasten it to the king stud with 10d common nails driven every 12" and toenail to the top plate.

4. Build the header to size and install, fastening it to the jack studs, king studs, and cripple studs using 16d common nails. Use a handsaw to cut through the bottom plate so it's flush with the inside faces of the jack studs. Remove the cutout portion.

5. Finish the walls with wallboard before installing the doors.

B. INSTALL PREHUNG FRENCH DOORS

1. Set the prehung door unit into the framed opening so the jamb edges are flush with the finished wall surfaces and the unit is centered from side to side.

2. Using a level, adjust the unit to plumb one of the side jambs. Starting near the top of the door, insert pairs of shims driven from opposite directions into the gap between the framing and the jamb. Slide the shims in until they are snug. Check the jamb to make sure it remains plumb and does not bow inward. Repeat with the other side, aligning them roughly with the shims of the first jamb.

Make sure the jamb is plumb, then anchor it with 8d finish nails. Leave the nail heads partially protruding so the jamb can be readjusted later, if necessary.

With doors closed, adjust the shims so the reveal between the doors is even. Shim the gap between the header and the head jamb (inset) to create a consistent reveal along the top when the doors are closed.

C. ANCHOR SHIMS

1. Working down along the jamb, continue to install shims near each hinge and near the floor.

2. Make sure the jamb is plumb, then anchor it with 8d finish nails driven through the jamb and shims and into the framing. Leave the nail heads partially protruding so the jamb can be adjusted later if necessary.

D. ADJUST REVEAL LINE & FINISH

1. With the doors closed, adjust the shims so the reveal between the doors is even and the tops of the doors align.

2. Shim the gap between the header and the head jamb to create a consistent reveal along the top when the doors are closed. Insert pairs of shims every 12". Drive 8d finish nails through the jambs and shims and into the faming members.

3. Drive the nails in, and then set them below the surface with a nail set. Cut off the shims flush with the wall surface, using a handsaw or utility knife. Hold the saw vertically to prevent damage to the door jamb or wall. Install the door casing.

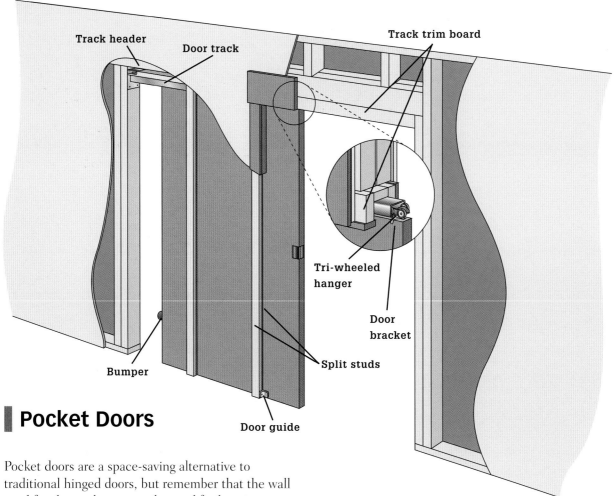

Track header Door track Track trim board

Tri-wheeled hanger

Door bracket

Split studs

Bumper

Door guide

Pocket Doors

Pocket doors are a space-saving alternative to traditional hinged doors, but remember that the wall used for the pocket cannot be used for hanging a custom closet section. Pocket door hardware kits can be adapted for almost any interior door. In this project, the frame kit includes an adjustable track, steel-clad split studs, and all the required hanging hardware. The latch hardware, jambs, and the door itself are all sold separately. Pocket door frames can also be purchased as preassembled units that can be easily installed into a rough opening.

Framing and installing a pocket door is not difficult in new construction or a major remodel. But retrofitting a pocket door in place of a standard door, or installing one in a wall without an existing door, is a major project that involves removing the wall material, framing the new opening, installing and hanging the door, and refinishing the wall. Hidden utilities, such as wiring, plumbing, and heating ducts, must be rerouted if encountered.

The rough opening for a pocket door is at least twice the width of a standard door opening. For this size of rough opening, use a built-up header (see page 115). Check with your local building department about sizing for your project.

Tools & Materials ▸

Tape measure	Door
Hammer	1¼" wallboard screws
Nail set	Wallboard materials
Screwdriver	Manufactured pocket
Level	door jambs (or cut
Drill	jambs from 1×
Hacksaw	lumber)
Wallboard tools	8d and 6d finish nails
2 × 4 lumber	1½" wood screws
8d, and 6d common	Door casing
nails	Wood finishing
Chalk lines	materials
Pocket door frame kit	

How to Install a Pocket Door

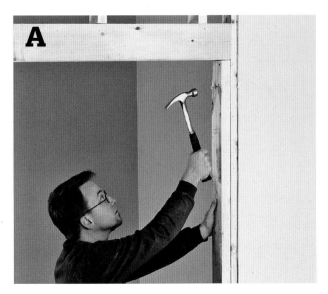

Mark each jack stud at the height of the door plus ¾" (or 1½" depending on the door clearance above the floor). Drive a nail into each jack stud, leaving about ⅛" protruding.

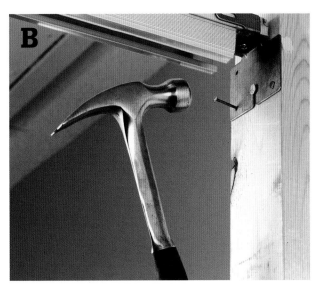

Set end brackets of track over nails in jack studs. Then drive 8d common nails through the remaining holes in the end bracket.

A. FRAME ROUGH OPENING

1. Prepare the project area and frame the rough opening to the manufacturer's recommended dimensions.
2. Measuring from the floor, mark each jack stud at the height of the door plus ¾ to 1½" (depending on the door clearance above the floor) for the overhead door track.
3. Drive a nail into each jack stud, centered on the mark. Leave about ⅛" of the nail protruding (for end brackets).

B. CUT & FASTEN TRACK

1. Remove the adjustable end bracket from the overhead door track.
2. Cut the wooden track header at the mark that matches your door size. Turn the track over and cut the metal track 1⅜" shorter than the wooden track header, using a hacksaw. Replace the end bracket.
3. Cut the side trim boards along the marks corresponding to your door size, being careful not to cut the metal track.
4. Set end brackets of track on the nails in the jack studs. Adjust track to level and set the nail. Then drive 8d common nails through the remaining holes in end brackets.

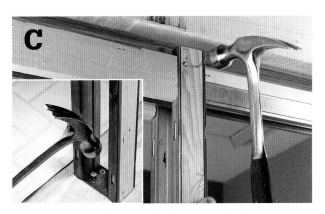

Butt split stud pair against the door track trim board and fasten it to the track header using 6d common nails.

C. INSTALL SPLIT STUDS

1. Snap chalk lines on the floor across the opening, and even with the sides of the rough opening.
2. Tap floor plate spacers into bottom ends of pairs of steel-clad split studs. Butt one split stud pair against the door track trim board, check it for plumb, and fasten it to the track header using 6d common nails.
3. Center the other split stud pair in the "pocket" and fasten it to the track header.
4. Plumb the split studs again and attach them to floor with 8d common nails or 2 screws driven through spacer plates.

Install wallboard with 1¼" wallboard screws. Do not finish seams until the door has been installed and aligned.

Fasten the strike-side jamb to the jack stud, using 8d finish nails. Shim the jamb to plumb as necessary.

Tri-wheeled hanger

Lock arm

Set the door in the frame, aligning the hangers with the door brackets. Raise the door and press each hanger into the bracket until it snaps into place.

D. INSTALL WALLBOARD

Install wallboard over the pocket to the edge of the opening. You may want to leave the wallboard off one side of the wall to allow for door adjustment. Do not finish wallboard until the door has been completely installed and adjusted. Use 1¼" wallboard screws, which will not protrude into the pocket.

E. INSTALL STRIKE-SIDE JAMB

1. Cut the strike-side jamb to length and width.
2. Fasten it to the jack stud, using 8d finish nails, shimming jamb to plumb as necessary.

F. INSTALL DOOR

1. Paint or stain the door as desired. *Note: For some door handles and latch hardware, you may need to notch the door before finishing.*

2. When the door has dried, attach two door brackets to the top of the door, using included screws driven through pilot holes.
3. Install the rubber bumper to the rear edge of the door with its included screw (follow the manufacturer's recommendation for bumper placement).
4. Slide two tri-wheeled hangers into the overhead door track.
5. Set the door in the frame, aligning the hangers with the door brackets. Then raise the door and press each hanger into the door bracket until it snaps into place. Close the lock arm over the hanger.
6. Close the door and adjust the hanger nuts to fine-tune the door height so the door is parallel with the strike-side jamb from top to bottom.

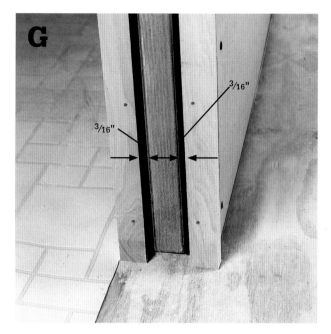

Fasten each split jamb to the front edge of the split stud, using 8d finish nails. Maintain a $^3/_{16}$" clearance on both sides of door.

G. INSTALL SPLIT JAMBS

1. Measure and cut the split jambs to size. With the door open all the way, hold the jambs against the split studs to confirm that the door is flush with jambs. If necessary, shim between the bumper and door until the door is flush.
2. Fasten each split jamb to front edge of split stud, using 8d finish nails. Maintain $^3/_{16}$" clearance on both sides of door.

H. INSTALL SPLIT HEAD JAMB

1. Measure and cut the split head jambs to size.
2. Use $1^1/_2$" wood screws driven through countersunk pilot holes to attach the head jamb on the side that has access to the lock arm of the hangers. This allows for easy removal of the door.
3. Attach the other head jamb using 6d finish nails. Maintain $^3/_{16}$" clearance on each side of the door.

I. FINISHING TOUCHES

1. Install the included door guides on both sides of the door near the floor at the mouth of the pocket.
2. Install the latch hardware according to the manufacturer directions.
3. Finish the wallboard and install casing around the door.
4. Fill all nails holes with wood putty, then paint or stain the jambs and casing as desired.

Attach the head jamb on the side that has access to the lock arm of the hangers with $1^1/_2$" wood screws driven through countersunk pilot holes.

Install the door latch hardware according to the manufacturer instructions.

Bifold Doors

Bifold doors provide easy access to a closet without requiring much clearance for opening. Most home centers stock kits that include two pairs of prehinged doors, a head track, and all the necessary hardware and fasteners. Typically, the doors in these kits have predrilled holes for the pivot and guide posts. Hardware kits also are sold separately for custom projects. There are many types of bifold door styles, so be sure to read and follow the manufacturer instructions for the product you use.

Tools & Materials ▶

Tape measure
Level
Circular saw
Straightedge
  (optional)
Drill
Plane
Screwdriver
Hacksaw

Prehinged bifold doors
Head track
Mounting hardware
Panhead screws
Flathead screws

How to Install a Bifold Door

A. MOUNT HEAD TRACK

1. Check to make sure the opening has square corners, a level header, and straight jambs. To operate properly, bifold doors must be hung level and plumb in the opening.
2. Cut the head track to the width of the opening, using a hacksaw.
3. Insert the roller mounts into the track, and then position the track in the opening.
4. Fasten the track to the header, using panhead screws.
5. Measure and mark each side jamb at the floor for the anchor bracket, so the center of the bracket aligns exactly with the center of the head track.
6. Fasten the brackets in place with flathead screws.

B. INSTALL POSTS

1. Check the height of the doors in the opening, and trim if necessary. Make minor adjustments using a plane, and larger alterations using a circular saw and straightedge guide to ensure a clean, straight cut.
2. Insert a pivot post into predrilled holes at the top and bottom of the two jamb-side doors, at the jamb side of each door. Make sure the pivot posts fit snugly.
3. Insert a guidepost into the predrilled holes at the top of both leading doors. Make sure the guideposts fit snugly.

C. HANG DOOR

1. Fold one pair of doors closed and lift into position, inserting the pivot and guideposts into the head track.
2. Slip the bottom pivot post into the anchor bracket. Repeat for the other pair of doors.
3. Close the doors and check for equal spacing along the side jambs and down the center. To align the doors, adjust the top and bottom pivots following manufacturer instructions.

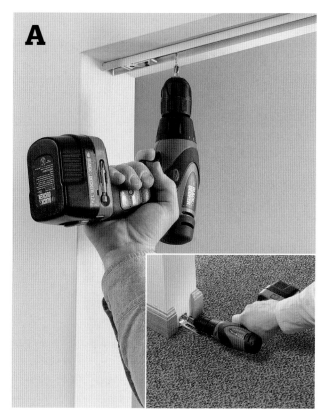

Fasten the track to the header with panhead screws. Fasten brackets to the side jambs with flathead screws.

Insert pivot posts into predrilled holes at the bottoms and tops of doors. Insert guide posts at the tops of the leading doors.

Lift doors into position, inserting the pivot and guide posts into the head track.

Ventilation Systems

How to Install Ventilation Fans

A. MARK & CUT THE FIRST WALL

1. Mark an area on the wall for the vent, making sure there are no studs or other obstructions in this area. Follow manufacturer instructions for exact placement—some models have cords that must be plugged into an outlet, so the vent must be close enough to the wall to operate correctly.
2. Hold the fan or vent against the wall and trace around the part of the unit that must fit into the wall. Make sure any power cords are on the downside (unless specified otherwise by manufacturer).
3. Cut out the opening with a small wallboard saw, cutting inside the pencil line.

B. MARK & CUT THE SECOND WALL

1. Trace the edge of the cutout onto the inside of the other wallboard. Use a ruler to extend from the cutline to the other wall and make marks on either side of the ruler.
2. Use a small nail to create a few small holes in the interior of the wall at marks.
3. Walk around to the other side of the wall to inspect your pinhole marks from the exterior of the second wall. Hold the other side of the fan up to the circle and trace a cutline. This cutline should follow the nail holes.
4. Cut the opening with a small drywall saw, cutting inside the pencil line.

5. Insert the first half of the fan into the cutout opening, following manufacturer instructions.
6. Insert the second half into the cutout opening on the other side of the wall, fitting the two sides together in the center of the wall.

C. INSTALL FAN

1. Mark the location of the wall anchors.
2. Drill the holes for the anchors with a $^3\!/_{16}$" drill bit.
3. Install the wall anchors.
4. Screw the grille down at wall anchor locations.
5. Repeat for the fan on the other wall.

> ## Tip ▸
>
> If you have a power cord, run it along the baseboard to the electrical outlet using cord control clips or a cord channel.

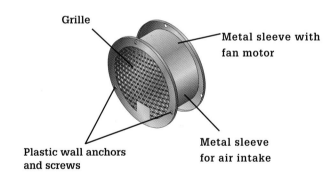

Grille

Metal sleeve with fan motor

Plastic wall anchors and screws

Metal sleeve for air intake

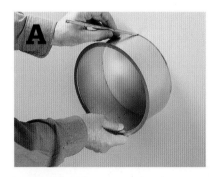

Mark the wall where there are no studs, and then hold the vent up to the wall and trace around it for a cut line.

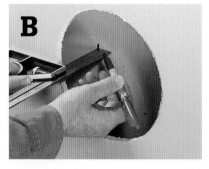

Trace the cut line to the interior of the other side of the wall.

Drill placement holes using a $^1\!/_{32}$" drill bit.

Baskets

Baskets offer well-ventilated storage for blankets and clothing. They are also convenient solutions for small knickknacks, craft supplies, and small projects (such as knitting or crocheting). Baskets on tracks ensure a permanent spot for your items—and they are as easy to install as they are to use. Are you ready? As soon as you can say 1-2-3 you'll have your very own sliding baskets in your custom closet!

Tools & Materials ▸

Screwdriver
Tape measure

Gliding basket kit (with fastening hardware)

How to Install a Gliding Basket

Measure the width and depth of the space you want to insert a basket.

A. Measure the space in between two verticals. Baskets with tracks are sold at most home centers now. Standard widths are 16 and 24". Standard heights are 5 and 10". Standard depths are 12 and 14".

B. Holding basket in space, align a track and make marks for its location on verticals. Fasten track to vertical at this location following manufacturer instructions. Some tracks have pins that simply press into predrilled holes on vertical, while others use Euro or barrel screws.

C. Slide basket into place over tracks. Check for level, and adjust if necessary.

With a screwdriver, fasten Euro screws through the track and into the vertical. Follow manufacturer instructions (often, the Euro screws fit directly into the predrilled holes in vertical).

Simply slide the basket into place over track, following manufacturer instructions.

Vertical Spacers

Everyone has some of those awkward items that don't seem to fit anywhere, and they are the items that always end up tucked away into a corner where they're hard to reach—or find!—at that moment when you most need them. Vertical spacers are a nifty little trick to keep those awkward, "often-forgot-about" items neat and tidy year-round. They're the perfect solution for everything from wrapping paper rolls, baseball bats, and extra golf clubs to equestrian crops and hockey sticks.

Our vertical spacers are designed to fit right into a custom closet design—between two verticals. The average width between verticals is 24", so our plan specs match that. The height is determined by the height of the items being stored. Our design is 30", which accommodates most wrapping paper rolls. We use ¾"-thick melamine stock.

Tools, Materials & Cutting List ▸

Tape measure
Handheld screwdriver
Circular saw with
 melamine blade
Drill and bit for KD
 fittings
Rubber mallet
KDs
KD screws and dowels

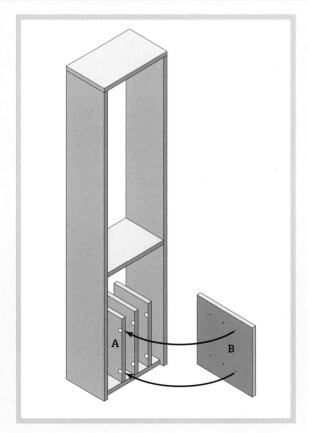

Key	Part	Dimension	Pcs.	Material
A	Shelf	¾ × 13¼ × 29¼"	1	Melamine shelf stock with predrilled holes
B	Front panel	30 x 24"	1	¾"-thick MDF sheet front panel
C	Verticals	29¼ × 13¼"	3	¾" melamine
D	KDs		8	With screws

How to Make Vertical Spacers

Cut verticals to size, making sure you account for the top shelf's ¾" thickness.

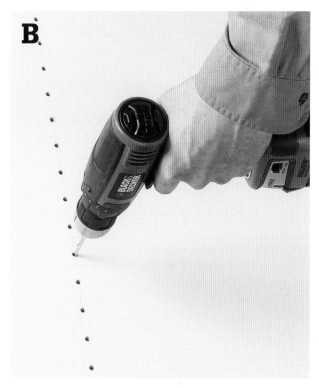

Drill holes on the inside of front panel at pencil marks.

A. MEASURE AND CUT VERTICALS

1. Measure and cut vertical spacers to size (13¼ × 29¼"). Use a circular saw with a melamine blade. Cut at ³/₈" on center of pin holes from top edge. For a closet unit with 14" verticals, purchase 14 or 16" shelf stock and cut down to size of 13¼".
2. If you're not using shelf stock with predrilled holes, drill shelf-pin holes along both sides of each vertical (see page 46).

B. MEASURE AND CUT FRONT PANEL

1. Measure and cut the front panel to size (24 × 30"), using a circular saw.
2. Drill holes along the inside of the front panel (see page 126 for drilling guide) for spacers to fasten to.

C. INSTALL VERTICAL SPACERS

1. Slide spacers into place at desired locations. Align front panel flush with verticals.
2. Adjust spacers so they are on center to predrilled holes in front panel. Mark two locations on each spacer side for KDs—one toward the top and one toward the bottom.
3. Rout out KD holes on vertical spacers at marks, and according to manufacturer instructions.
4. Tap KDs into holes with a rubber mallet.
5. Fasten screws into predrlled holes in front panel, leaving them sticking out about ⅛", so KDs can fit over them.
6. Slide spacers into place with KDs fitting over screws. Lock down the KDs.

Align front panel and vertical spacers and mark KD locations on the vertical spacers.

Closet Island

In the age of huge walk-ins, the closet island has presented a unique way to use the otherwise dead space in the center of a large, walkin closet. This project not only offers extra storage, it also offers a convenient space to lay out the day's clothing and accessories. The slight overhang allows for short stools or a bench to be tucked away or called into use for getting ready in the morning. The island encourages you to take your time and truly enjoy your closet.

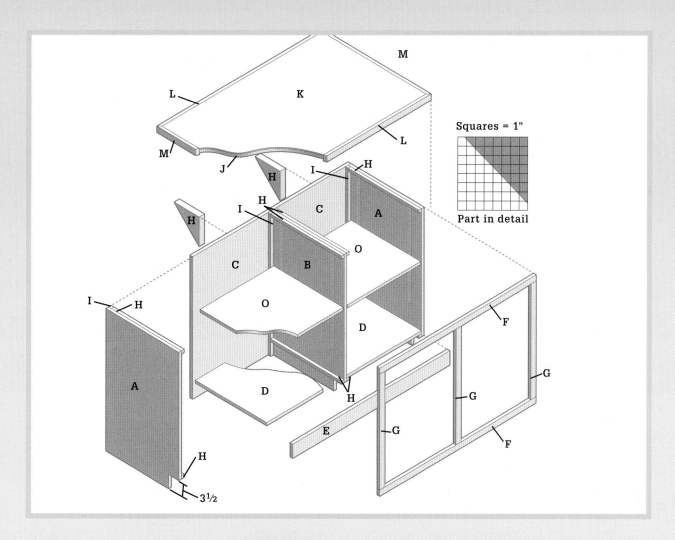

Squares = 1"

Part in detail

Tools

Tape measure
Circular Saw
Combination square
Jigsaw
Clamps
Drill
Hammer
Sandpaper
Orbital sander
Miter Saw
Nail set

Materials

Wood glue
#6 wood screws (1", 1½")
½" tacks
4d finish nails
(8) 24" shelf standards
Shelf standard supports
Contact cement
Finishing materials

Cutting List

Key	Part	Dimension	Pcs.	Material
A	End	⅝ × 21½ × 35"	2	Pine panel
B	Divider	⅝ × 21½ × 35"	1	Pine panel
C	Back	⅝ × 22⅛ × 35"	2	Pine panel
D	Bottom	⅝ × 21⅛ × 21½"	1	Pine
E	Toe kick	¾ × 3½ × 44¼"	1	Pine
F	Rail	¾ × 1½ × 44¼"	2	Pine
G	Stile	¾ × 1½ × 28½"	3	Pine
H	Horizontal cleat	¾ × ¾ × 20¾"	8	Molding
I	Vertical cleat	¾ × ¾ × 35"	4	Molding
J	Substrate	¾ × 30½ × 46½"	1	Particleboard
K	Top	¼ × 30½ × 46½"	1	Tileboard
L	Long edge	¾ × 1½ × 32"	2	Pine
M	Short edge	¾ × 1½ × 32"	2	Pine
N	Support	1½ × 7¼ × 7¼"	2	Pine
O	Shelf	⅝ × 20½ × 20½"	2	Pine panel

How to Make an Island

Cut the toe-kick notches into the ends and divider using a jigsaw.

Gang the cleats together while drilling countersunk pilot holes.

A. CUT THE ENDS & DIVIDER

1. Cut the ends and divider to size from pine panels, using a circular saw.
2. Measure and mark the 3"-wide × 3½"-tall toe-kick notches on the lower front corner of all three pieces using a combination square. This notch allows you to approach the cabinet without stubbing your toes against the bottom.
3. Clamp each piece to your work surface, and cut out the toe-kick notches using a jigsaw.

B. PREPARE THE CLEATS

The cleats reinforce the internal joints of the cabinet. Countersunk pilot holes are drilled through each cleat in two directions and are offset so the screws won't hit one another.

1. Cut the horizontal and the verticals cleats to length from ¾ × ¾" stop molding.
2. Clamp the vertical cleats together so the ends are flush, and mark four pilot hole locations along the length of each cleat. Drill countersunk pilot holes at each marked location.
3. Remove the clamps and give each cleat a quarter turn. Reclamp the cleats, then mark and drill the second set of offset pilot holes. Repeat the process for the horizontal cleats, drilling three holes through one edge of each cleat and two offset holes through an adjacent edge.

C. ASSEMBLE THE ENDS & DIVIDER

1. Align a vertical cleat along the inside back edge of one of the ends. Align the pilot holes so the back can be attached through the offset holes.
2. Apply glue and fasten the cleat to the end with countersunk 1" screws. Attach vertical cleats to the inside face of the other end, and to both back edges of the divider. Attach the horizontal cleats to the ends and divider, using glue and 1" screws.

D. ATTACH THE SHELF STANDARDS

1. Cut a 15 × 30" template from scrap particleboard or heavy-stock cardboard. Make sure the standards are properly aligned in the same direction so the holes for the supports line up.
2. Place the template on the lower horizontal cleat, and center the template between the vertical cleat and the front edge. Measure 2" up from the bottom edge along each side of the template and make a reference mark.
3. Place a standard against each edge of the template and adjust so the bottom of the standard is on the 2" mark. Nail the standards in place with the provided nails.
4. Repeat for the other end, and on both faces of the divider.

Center a marked template between the cleats to uniformly attach the shelf standards.

E. ASSEMBLE THE CABINET

1. Cut the backs, bottoms, and toe-kick to size, and sand the edges smooth.
2. Cut $\frac{3}{4} \times \frac{3}{4}$" notches in the back corners of each bottom to accommodate the vertical cleats.
3. Stand one end and the divider upright on their front edges. Position a bottom piece against the lower horizontal cleats. Use bar clamps to hold the assembly in place, and attach the bottom with glue and 1" screws driven through the pilot holes in each cleat. Position the remaining bottom and end in place, and attach the bottom to the cleats.
4. Attach the back pieces one at a time, using glue and 1" screws driven through the vertical cleats inside the cabinet. Make sure each back piece is aligned with its inside edge flush against a marked reference center line on the divider. Check frequently for square, and use pipe clamps to hold the pieces in position as you attach them.
5. Carefully turn the assembly over, and fasten the toe-kick in place with glue and 4d finish nails.

F. ASSEMBLE THE FACE FRAME

1. Cut the rails and stiles to size, and sand them smooth. Position the top rail so the top edges and corners are flush, and attach with glue and finish nails. Attach the stiles so the outside edges are flush with the end faces and centered on the divider. Finally, attach the bottom rail.
2. Reinforce the joints by drilling pilot holes through the rails into the ends of each stile and securing with 4d finish nails.
3. Use an orbital sander to smooth the face frame and the joints between stile and rails. By sanding the stiles before the rails, you can avoid cross-sanding marks at the joints.

Clamp the back to the divider along the centerline, and adjust when attaching to the end.

Arrange the toe-kick so the corners and edges are flush, and attach to the divider and ends with glue and 4d finish nails.

Sand the rails after the stiles to avoid cross-sanding marks at the toe-kick joints.

Clamp scrap boards to the tileboard to distribute pressure and establish good contact.

Attach the supports to the back from inside the cabinet using glue and screws.

G. BUILD THE COUNTERTOP

1. Cut the particleboard substrate, tileboard top, long edges, and short edges to size. Make sure the top fits perfectly over the substrate, and trim if necessary.
2. Miter-cut the ends of the long edges and short edges at 45° angles to fit around the countertop.
3. Apply contact cement to the substrate, and clamp the tileboard top in place, using scrap wood under the clamps to distribute pressure and ensure even contact with the cement.
4. Unclamp and flip the assembly on its top when dry. Arrange the long and short edges around the countertop so the top surface will be flush with the tops of the edge pieces. Glue and clamp the edges in place. Drill pilot holes and drive 4d finish nails through the edges into the substrate.

H. ATTACH THE COUNTERTOP & SHELVES

1. Cut the shelves from pine panels and the supports from 2 × 8 dimensional pine. Round the cut corners at the long ends of each diagonal, using a jigsaw or a sander to soften the profile of the supports.
2. Mark a line on the top edge of the back, 11" in from each end. Position the supports so they are centered on the lines. Drill pilot holes through the back and attach the supports with glue and 1½" countersunk screws driven from the inside of the cabinet.

3. Center the countertop from side to side on the cabinet with a 1" overhang on the front. Attach with glue and 1½" screws driven up through the top horizontal cleats. Insert supports into the shelf standards at the desired height, and install the shelves inside the cabinet with the grain running left to right.
4. Recess all visible nail heads with a nail set, and fill the holes with putty. Sand all surfaces, outer edges, and corners smooth.
5. Finish the island with a light stain and apply a nontoxic topcoat. We used a traditional American pine finish.

> ### Tip ▸
>
> The back, end, divider, bottom, and shelf pieces used in this project are constructed from ⅝" edge-glued ponderosa pine panels, available at most building centers. This material, available in varying dimensions and thicknesses, is manufactured from small-width pine glued together under pressure. The result is a strong material that is slightly thinner than standard dimensional plywood. It features a distinctive paneled appearance, and since it is made entirely of one type of wood, exposed edges do not require veneer.

Drawer Components

Any drawer can be transformed into a custom jewelry and notions drawer by simply lining boxes with fabric. Small sections are perfect for jewelry, while slightly larger sections help organize scarves, socks, and lingerie. Not only is this level of organization and class a luxury addition to any closet, but it adds that final custom detail to be proud of. For smaller boxes we recommend using 10-ply poster board or bristol board. For large boxes use 14-ply or 16-ply board. You can also use purchased cardboard or wooden bandboxes.

Tools & Materials ▶

Disposable foam
    brush
Fabric glue
Spray adhesive
Mediumweight
    (firmly woven)
    fabrics for outer
    fabric and lining

Polyester fleece
1"-wide white tape
Artist knife
Chipboard or carboard

How to Make a Tray

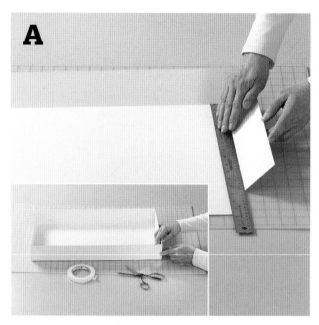

Fold scored edges up, using a roller to ensure a straight fold along reference line. (Inset) Tape sides together.

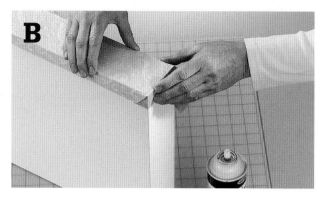

Apply spray adhesive to wrong side of fabric and fix tray.

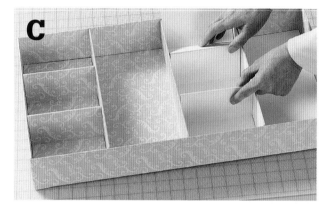

Test-fit inserts before applying line.

A. MAKE THE TRAY

1. Mark the sides of the box on outside of cardboard, using a pencil. Score along the marked lines, using straightedge and artist knife to cut cardboard lightly (do not cut through). Cut out corner areas of cardboard, using an artist knife.
2. Fold sides, supporting cardboard on straightedge or edge of table along scored line to keep folds straight.
3. Tape sides together, using white tape. Construct lid, using the same method as for the box, except make lid ¼" wider and longer than box measurements.

B. APPLY LINING TO TRAY

1. Apply spray adhesive to wrong side of fabric. Fix to the tray, wrapping 1" of fabric around ends and bottom. Miter corners on bottom of tray, and then fix to box with fabric glue (follow manufacturer instructions). Repeat for the remaining side piece.
2. Wrap remaining fabric to inside of tray, mitering corners on floor of tray. Fix to tray with fabric glue, following manufacturer instructions. Fix end and bottom pieces by wrapping the fabric around edge to inside. Seal raw edges of fabric with glue.

C. MAKE INSERTS

1. Sketch diagram showing size of sections and placement of dividers. Mark tray measurements on the sketch. Cut chipboard for the first divider, Mark foldlines on both sides of divider, and then label which direction the divider will be folded on each line.
2. Score along marked lines, using an artist knife and straightedge. If divider will be folded up, score bottom of divider (if it will be folded down, score the top).
3. Fold divider into the desired shape. Apply spray adhesive or diluted fabric glue to wrong side of fabric. Fix the fabric to the top of shaped divider. Wrap fabric around edges to underside of divider. Glue the fabric in place.
4. Glue the first divider in the tray. Measure sections and repeat steps, checking fit before covering with fabric.

Making a Jig for Straight Cuts ▸

In this book we suggest using a simple right-angle jig on several occasions. The jig ensures straight cuts.

Fasten cleat flush along the short factory edge, using glue and wood screws (driven through countersunk pilot holes so the screw heads are slightly below the surface). Make sure the cleat is straight and perfectly flush with base's edge.

If desired, mark the long factory edge so you'll know which one is your guide edge.

Cut base from ¾"-thick melamine stock. Keeping two perpendicular factory edges intact, cut the base about 12" wide and 2" longer than the width of your shelving stock. Cut a straight piece of 1 × 2 cleat to match width of base.

Using a Biscuit Joiner ▸

For making drawers (see page 10) we recommend using biscuits to join drawers and shelves on occasion. A biscuit joiner provides professional application of biscuits. This tool has a small circular blade tucked into a housing at the front of the saw. When you press the spring-loaded tool against the edge of a board, the self-registering blade emerges from the housing and engages the board edge, cutting a perfect slot.

Set the height of the fence on the biscuit joiner to one-half of the thickness of the material to be joined.

Turn the blade depth adjustment knob to the appropriate biscuit size for the project.

Clamp the first workpiece to a flat work surface, and align the registration mark on the biscuit joiner with the cutting line. Cut the first biscuit slot by pressing the joiner firmly into the edge of the workpiece, keeping a firm grip on both to avoid slipping out of alignment. Cut a slot in the mating workpiece the same way.

Resources

Specialty Hardware

BUILDEX
800-284-5339
E-Z Toggle, E-Z Ancor, drywall anchors, and self-drilling toggle bolts.

CALIFORNIA CLOSETS
800-274-6754
www.calclosets.com
Design consultation and custom installation.

CLOSET MASTERS
800-548-1868
Consumer sales for Häfele products.

EASY CLOSETS
800-910-0129
www.easyclosets.com
Closet accessories, precut corner shelves, closet kits (including modular hardware).

HÄFELE
800-423-3531
www.hafele.com
Closet hardware, connectors, wall rails and rail covers, and shelf supports for contractors. Consumers may purchase Häfele products at Closet Masters and KitchenSource.com (see individual listings above).

HILTI
800-879-8000
KwikTog (plastic) toggles, Toggler brand toggle bolts, and other Hilti anchors.

HOME DEPOT
800-553-3199
www.homedepot.com
Baskets, drawers, rods, closet accessories, closet kits (including modular hardware), melamine.

HVAC
877-711-4822
www.hvacquick.com
Ventilation fans.

IKEA
800-434-4532
www.IKEA-usa.com
Bookcase and corner bookcase combinations, drawer chests, wardrobe combinations, armoires, shoe racks, shelving, clothes rails, wire baskets, pants hangers, drawers with dividers, valet rods, drawer jewelry boxes, storage systems.

KITCHENSOURCE.COM
800-667-8721
Consumer sales for Häfele specialty products and closet accessories.

MOBILEFFE
www.mobileffe.com
info@mobileffe.com
Wardrobe and walk-in closet design.

ORGANIZE-IT
800-210-7712
www.organize-it.com
Closet accessories, wire shelving, closet kits.

POLIFORM
202-554-8658
www.poliform.net
Wardrobes and walk-in dressing room design.

SLIDING DOOR CO.
888-433-1333
www.slidingdoorco.com
Sliding (track) doors appropriate for closet applications.

TWIN CITIES CLOSETS
612-623-0987
www.twincitiesclosets.com
Custom design and installation services.

WOODCRAFT
www.woodcraft.com
800-535-4482

WOODHARBOR
641-423-0444
www.woodharbor.com
Doors and cabinetry.

Photo Credits

p. 4 / photo courtesy of California Closets
p. 6 (top left) / photo courtesy of Ikea
p. 6 (bottom left) / photo courtesy of California Closets
p. 6 (right) / photo courtesy of Mobileffe
p. 6 (right inset) / photo courtesy of Mobileffe
p. 7 (top) / photo courtesy of Ikea
p. 7 (lower left) / photo of Twin Cities Closets by Steve Galvin of CPi.
p. 7 (lower right) / photo courtesy of California Closets
p. 8 (top) / photo courtesy of Mobileffe
p. 8 (lower) / photo courtesy of Mobileffe
p. 9 (lower left) / photo by Eric Lamph for Sliding Door Co.
p. 9 (right) / photo Beateworks Inc. / Alamy
p. 10 (top) / photo courtesy of Mobileffe
p.10 (lower left and right) / photos courtesy of California Closets
p. 11 (top and bottom) / photos courtesy of California Closets
p. 12 / photo courtesy of California Closets
p. 13 (top left and right) / photos courtesy of California Closets
p. 13 (lower left and right) / photos courtesy of Organize-It
p. 50 / photo courtesy of Organize-It
p. 54 / photo courtesy of California Closets
p. 88 / photo courtesy of California Closets
p. 92 / photo courtesy of California Closets
p. 126 / photo courtesy of Woodharbor
p. 132 (top) / photo of Twin Cities Closets by Steve Galvin of CPi.
p. 132 (bottom) / photo courtesy of California Closets

Metric Conversions

Converting Measurements

To Convert:	To:	Multiply by:
Inches	Millimeters	25.4
Inches	Centimeters	2.54
Feet	Meters	0.305
Yards	Meters	0.914
Square inches	Square centimeters	6.45
Square feet	Square meters	0.093
Square yards	Square meters	0.836
Cubic inches	Cubic centimeters	16.4
Cubic feet	Cubic meters	0.0283
Cubic yards	Cubic meters	0.765
Ounces	Milliliters	30.0
Pints (U.S.)	Liters	0.473 (Imp. 0.568)
Quarts (U.S.)	Liters	0.946 (Imp. 1.136)
Gallons (U.S.)	Liters	3.785 (Imp. 4.546)
Ounces	Grams	28.4
Pounds	Kilograms	0.454

To Convert:	To:	Multiply by:
Millimeters	Inches	0.039
Centimeters	Inches	0.394
Meters	Feet	3.28
Meters	Yards	1.09
Square centimeters	Square inches	0.155
Square meters	Square feet	10.8
Square meters	Square yards	1.2
Cubic centimeters	Cubic inches	0.061
Cubic meters	Cubic feet	35.3
Cubic meters	Cubic yards	1.31
Milliliters	Ounces	.033
Liters	Pints (U.S.)	2.114 (Imp. 1.76)
Liters	Quarts (U.S.)	1.057 (Imp. 0.88)
Liters	Gallons (U.S.)	0.264 (Imp. 0.22)
Grams	Ounces	0.035
Kilograms	Pounds	2.2

Lumber Dimensions

Nominal - U.S.	Actual - U.S.	METRIC
1 × 2	¾ × 1½"	19 × 38 mm
1 × 3	¾ × 2½"	19 × 64 mm
1 × 4	¾ × 3½"	19 × 89 mm
1 × 5	¾ × 4½"	19 × 114 mm
1 × 6	¾ × 5½"	19 × 140 mm
1 × 7	¾ × 6¼"	19 × 159 mm
1 × 8	¾ × 7¼"	19 × 184 mm
1 × 10	¾ × 9¼"	19 × 235 mm
1 × 12	¾ × 11¼"	19 × 286 mm
1¼ × 4	1 × 3½"	25 × 89 mm
1¼ × 6	1 × 5½"	25 × 140 mm
1¼ × 8	1 × 7¼"	25 × 184 mm
1¼ × 10	1 × 9¼"	25 × 235 mm
1¼ × 12	1 × 11¼"	25 × 286 mm
1½ × 4	1¼ × 3½"	32 × 89 mm
1½ × 6	1¼ × 5½"	32 × 140 mm
1½ × 8	1¼ × 7¼"	32 × 184 mm
1½ × 10	1¼ × 9¼"	32 × 235 mm
1½ × 12	1¼ × 11¼"	32 × 286 mm
2 × 4	1½ × 3½"	38 × 89 mm
2 × 6	1½ × 5½"	38 × 140 mm
2 × 8	1½ × 7¼"	38 × 184 mm
2 × 10	1½ × 9¼"	38 × 235 mm
2 × 12	1½ × 11¼"	38 × 286 mm
3 × 6	2½ × 5½"	64 × 140 mm
4 × 4	3½ × 3½"	89 × 89 mm
4 × 6	3½ × 5½"	89 × 140 mm

Liquid Measurement Equivalents

1 Pint	= 16 Fluid Ounces	= 2 Cups
1 Quart	= 32 Fluid Ounces	= 2 Pints
1 Gallon	= 128 Fluid Ounces	= 4 Quarts

Converting Temperatures

Convert degrees Fahrenheit (F) to degrees Celsius (C) by following this simple formula: Subtract 32 from the Fahrenheit temperature reading. Then, multiply that number by 5/9. For example, 77°F - 32 = 45. 45 × 5/9 = 25°C.

To convert degrees Celsius to degrees Fahrenheit, multiply the Celsius temperature reading by 9/5. Then, add 32. For example, 25°C × 9/5 = 45. 45 + 32 = 77°F.

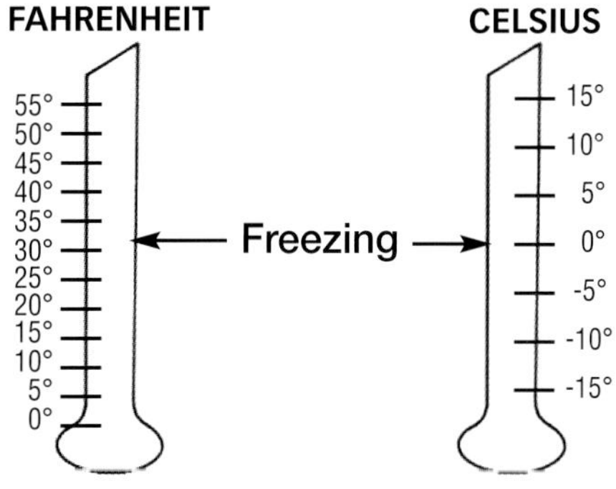

Index

Also From CREATIVE PUBLISHING international

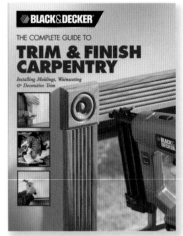

ISBN 1-58923-248-8

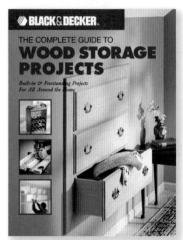

ISBN 1-58923-261-5

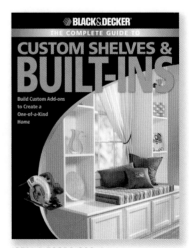

ISBN 1-58923-303-4

Creative Publishing international